THE POCKET GUIDE TO SEASHELLS OF THE NORTHERN HEMISPHERE

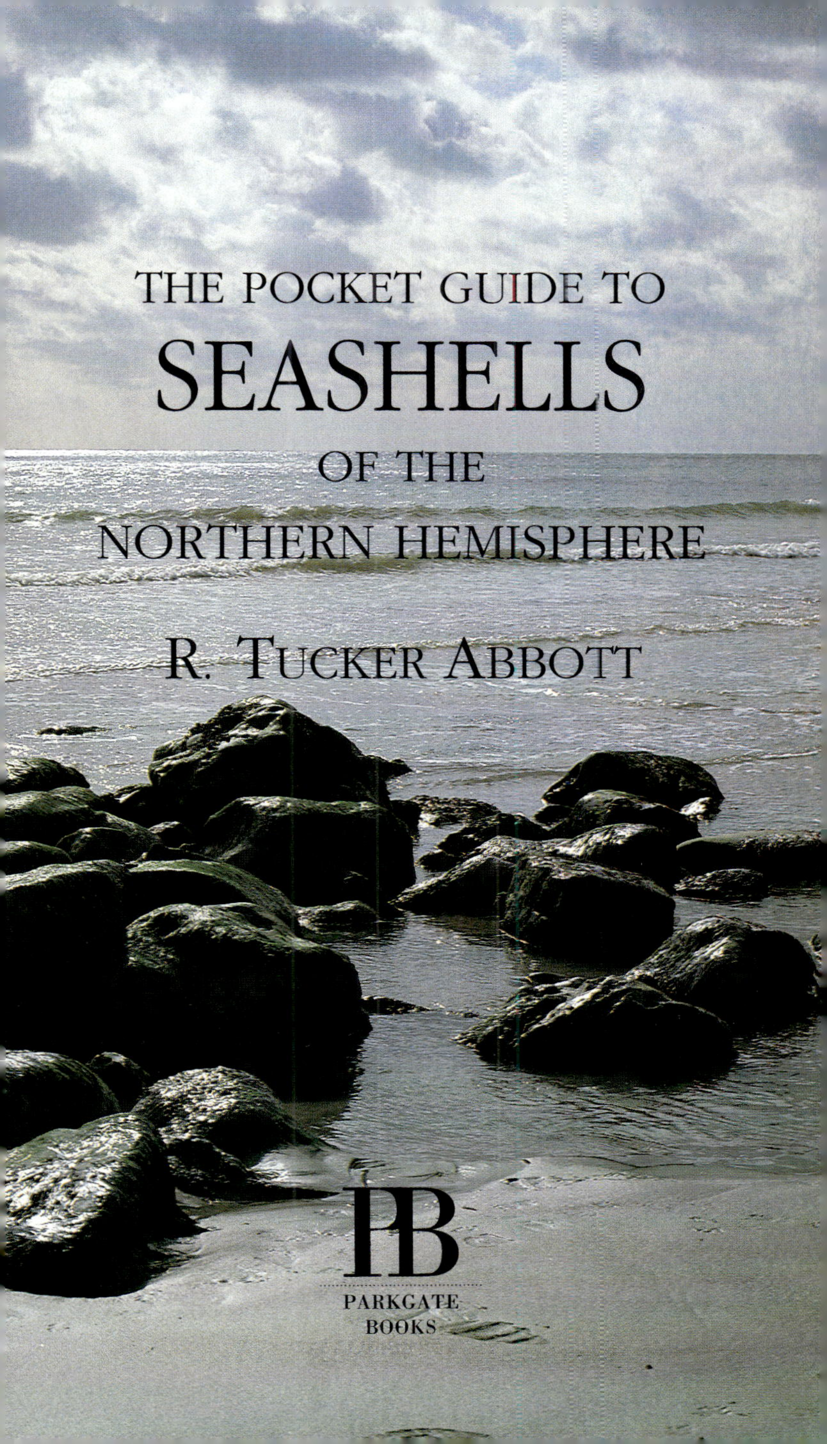

THE POCKET GUIDE TO SEASHELLS OF THE NORTHERN HEMISPHERE

R. TUCKER ABBOTT

PB
PARKGATE
BOOKS

First published in 1990

This edition published in 1998 by
Parkgate Books Ltd
Kiln House
210 New Kings Road
London SW6 4NZ
Great Britain

9 8 7 6 5 4 3 2 1

First published by Dragon's World Ltd in 1990 at £6.95

Editor: Diana Steedman
Designer: David Hunter
Editorial Director: Pippa Rubinstein

British Library Cataloguing in Publication Date:
A catalogue record for this book is available from the British Library.

ISBN 1 85585 544 5

Printed and bound in Italy

Contents

Introduction

For our great grandparents conchology, the study of shells and shellfish, was a pleasant and inspirational pastime that taught them about newly discovered shells from exotic seas. The bounties of nature were for the taking. But, with man's burgeoning populations, and the pollution of our shorelines, the modern study of shellfish, malacology, has developed to help combat the effects of oil spills, toxic drainage and other radical disturbances to the ecology of the world's molluscs.

The Phylum Mollusca

The phylum Mollusca includes seashells, squid and octopuses, as well as terrestrial and freshwater snails and clams, and outnumbers all the vertebrate species. The estimated 80,000 species of molluscs are a main source of food for fish, birds and man. Along our sandy or rocky shores they dominate marine life. Their populations are a barometer of the health of our seas.

The Arctic Ocean and the warmer seas that border it are a natural path for the interchange of circumpolar species. But the further south one goes, the more separate and distinct become the faunas in the warmer waters that are isolated by continental masses. While the life cycle of many snails and clams includes free-swimming stages that permit far-flung distributions, there are many molluscs that lay stationary egg capsules or give birth to live, crawling young. These different patterns of shell populations eventually lead to subspecies unique to small, isolated places.

This pocket guide offers a selection of the most frequently encountered types of molluscs found in the northern Pacific and Atlantic. Three major regions are covered: the north eastern Pacific from the Aleutian Islands and Alaska, south to Oregon; the north western Atlantic from Labrador to approximately Virginia; and the north eastern Atlantic from Scandinavia to Portugal.

How and Where Shells Live

Water temperature, substrate and wave action are the three primary factors influencing the nature of molluscan populations. Shorelines in Arctic and boreal regions are largely destitute of shells because of the grinding effect of seasonal ice cover. Offshore and under the ice there is a fairly rich fauna. In more temperate waters, protected back bays and tidepools along rocky coasts teem with marine life, although the number of species is relatively low.

Understanding the various species' habitat preferences makes locating them much easier. Some periwinkles and dogwinkles are hidden under festoons of rock-clinging algae; other snails are found only among clusters of barnacles and mussels; and the mud-loving nassa snails abound on intertidal flats. An old floating log, when broken apart, may reveal several species of wood-boring bivalves, and clinging to the underside of some sea stars and sea-urchins may be found tiny parasitic snails and clams. In identifying species it should be realized that in some cases certain species change shape as they grow older. Some univalves develop a thickened or expanded outer lip when they reach maturity. Diet and water conditions, as well as boring sponges and marauding crabs and fish, can alter the condition of the shell.

The Eastern Pacific, or western coast of North America, is bounded by the Arctic Sea where about 110 species can be obtained only by dredging from a boat or investigating wearing winter scuba gear. Southward, in the Aleutian subprovince, collecting improves and many species common to northern Japan and southern Alaska are readily obtained in shallow water. Below this is the Oregonian Province, one of the richest areas in the world for numbers of molluscan specimens. The temperate waters from northern British Columbia to Oregon and the northern sections of California are rich in rock-dwelling limpets, dogwinkles and mussels.

On the eastern coast of North America, the inhospitable shores of Hudson Bay, Labrador, Greenland and northern Iceland are relatively barren, although offshore waters support a respectable community of polar species. The Acadian subprovince, extending from Newfoundland and the Maritime Provinces south to Cape Cod, is fairly rich in shallow-water and shore species. There is a vast variation in habitats, from the extensive, intertidal mud flats of the Bay of Fundy to the gravel bottoms of Georges Banks and the sandy beaches of Cape Cod.

Western Europe, or the Eastern Atlantic, is also a mixture of major faunal elements. The conditions in northern Scandinavia and the Shetland Islands are as severe as those in northern Alaska. The Celtic Province, encompassing the British Isles, the Baltic Sea and France, is much richer and, indeed, has some elements that have invaded from the warmer Mediterranean Province, especially around northern Portugal. Occasionally, warmer-water, pelagic species are wafted on to the southern shores of England.

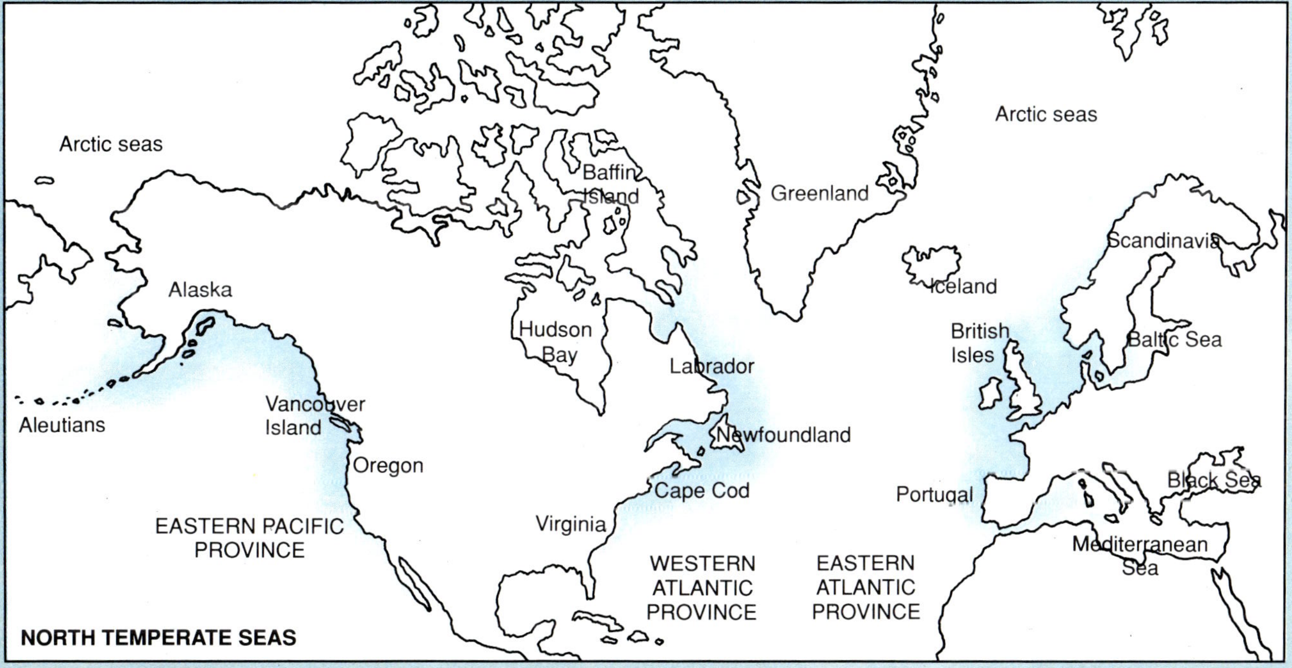
Arctic seas
Arctic seas
Baffin Island
Greenland
Scandinavia
Alaska
Iceland
Hudson Bay
British Isles
Baltic Sea
Labrador
Aleutians
Vancouver Island
Newfoundland
Oregon
Black Sea
Cape Cod
Portugal
Virginia
EASTERN PACIFIC PROVINCE
Mediterranean Sea
WESTERN ATLANTIC PROVINCE
EASTERN ATLANTIC PROVINCE
NORTH TEMPERATE SEAS

Common to most of these provinces in the northern hemisphere are many species of pelagic squids and tiny pteropod gastropods, all of which serve as an important source of food for fish and whales. Many shell-less sea-slugs, or nudibranchs, are common to England and New England. On the deep slopes of the continents, at many hundreds of feet in depth, there are many species of molluscs that have a circumpolar distribution because of the similar dark, cold conditions around the globe at those high latitudes.

Collecting Shells

While modest collecting of live specimens has less effect than nature's normal pruning by predation, aging and natural ecological changes, today there are more and more naturalists who prefer to hunt with camera or observe molluscs at close range in aquariums. But well-executed surveys and censuses must be backed by a sampling of correctly identified specimens. Provided you take only what you need, building a personal, well-documented shell collection is a pleasure and a useful project.

Shells with soft parts may be cleaned by boiling them in water for five minutes or placing them in a plastic, open bag in the microwave oven set on high for two minutes. The best preservative for very small shells or large soft parts is 70% grain alcohol. Formalin, unless well-buffered, will etch and eventually dissolve calcium carbonate shells. Geographical and ecological data should be recorded in a catalogue and be repeated on good label paper to accompany the india ink-numbered shells. Arrange the collection in phylogenetic order, the sequence in which most shell guides, including this one, are organized.

How to Use this Book

This pocket guide provides photographic colour reference along with descriptive details covering special features, measurement and distribution for over 370 shells which can be found along the west coast and the eastern seaboard of the United States, and the northern and western coasts of Europe. The various families of molluscs are arranged in a standard biological order, with the more primitive, or simpler, species presented first, followed by the more advanced kinds. But this is still only a small proportion of the vast array of molluscs that exist. To serve as a bridge to the more complete works, a bibliography appears on page 172, while the glossary on pages 11-14 defines the words used in the descriptions.

Glossary

While many unfamiliar nouns and adjectives used in conchology may be found in dictionaries, for the convenience of collectors and observers in the field, a brief glossary of the most frequently used words in our shell descriptions is included here. Those words *italicised* are also defined.

Adductor muscle (in *bivalves*). Large muscle inside the shell that closes the two valves.
Anterior end Front end; in *univalves*, the head or *siphonal end*; in *bivalves*, where the foot usually protrudes.
Aperture The opening in the last *whorl*, providing an outlet for the head and foot of a snail.
Apex The first-formed, narrow end of a snail shell, usually of several *whorls*.
Axial Parallel to the lengthwise axis of a shell; *suture* to suture features.

Base The lower *siphonal end* of the body or last *whorl*; opposite the *apex*.
Beak (or *umbo*) The first formed part of a *bivalve's* valve, usually above the *hinge*.
Bivalve A member of the class Bivalvia (or Pelecypoda), such as a clam or oyster.
Body whorl The largest and most recently formed *whorl*.
Boreal Relating to the northern climatic zone.
Byssus A clump of horny threads spun by the foot of a *bivalve* and used for attachment.

Callus A thickening, usually of shelly material.
Cancellate Marked by crossing lines, like latticework.
Chitinous Horny or corneous, usually soft and flexible material making up an *operculum*.
Chondrophore Spoon-shaped shelf in the *hinge* of a *bivalve*.
Circumpolar Found around either the North or South Pole.
Columella The solid pillar at the *axis* of the *univalve* shell, around which the *whorls* grow.
Concentric Sculpturing of ridges, ribs or threads, or colour markings, running parallel to the margins of a *bivalve* or *operculum*.

Dextral Right-handed or of *whorls* growing clockwise. *Aperture* at right if *apex* is held uppermost.

Escutcheon A smooth, long surface on the upper margin of the *valve* of a *bivalve* behind the *ligament*.

Fimbriated Having thin, wavy, rough, fringed borders.
Fusiform Shaped like a spindle, swollen in the centre, narrow as each end.

Gape Opening between the margins of the *valves* when the *bivalve* is shut.
Gastropod A mollusc possessing a single shell (*univalve*).
Globular Bulbous, or shaped like a round globe.

Head scar Muscular attachment scar inside a limpet.
Hinge Top margin of a *bivalve* where shelly teeth interlock.

Inner lip The wall on the body *whorl* opposite the outer lip of the *aperture*.
Intertidal Area between high and low tide mark.

Keyhole Small hole at top of some limpet snails.

Ligament An internal or external horny band, usually behind the *beaks*, holding the clam's *valves* together or ajar.
Lira(ae) Fine, raised lines or teeth, usually spiral in nature.
Lunule A long or heart-shaped impression on the upper margin of the *valves* in front of the clam's *beaks*, one half being in each valve.

Mantle Soft, fleshy organ producing shelly material..
Millepore growths Hard encrusting colonies of fire coral.
Multispiral Of many *whorls*, as in some *opercula*.

Nuclear whorl The first and smallest *whorl* in the *apex*.
Nucleus The centre or beginning point, usually in an *operculum* or *spire*.

Operculum(opercula) A 'trapdoor' attached to the foot of a snail that, when withdrawn, helps to seal the *aperture*.
Outer lip Final edge of the body *whorl*, often thickened in adults.
Ovate Oval-shaped.

Pallial line A scar line on the inside of a clam's shell, where the *mantle* muscles are attached.
Pallial sinus An embayment in the *pallial line* indicating where the *siphon*-retracting muscles are attached to the shell.

Parietal wall The area on the body *whorl* on the *columella* side of the *aperture* (or *inner lip*).
Paucispiral Having few *whorls*, as in *Littorina* opercula.
Pelagic Living or occurring in the upper waters of the ocean.
Periostracum The *chitinous* layer covering the outer shell, sometimes thin, thick or hairy.
Plankton Small animals and plants normally floating in the open ocean.
Prodissoconch Minute, first-formed shell on the clam's *beak*.

Radial Sculpturing or colour rays (in *bivalves*) or ribs (in *univalves*) running parallel to the main *axis*, from *suture* to suture.
Resilium A horny, pad-like cushion located on the *bivalve's chondrophore*.
Reticulations Squarish pattern formed by the crossing of concentric and axial sculpturing.

Sculpture Relief pattern on the shell surface; ribs, spines.
Sinistral "Left-handed" or of *whorls* growing anti-clockwise.
Siphon Tube-like extension for passage of water.
Siphonal end Narrow front end of a shell where the siphon is located.
Spiral Sculpturing or colouring encircling the *whorls* parallel to the *sutures*.
Spire The *whorls* at the apical end, exclusive of the last whorl.
Substrate The bottom or supporting surface.
Subtidal Below the low tide mark.
Suture Continuous line on the shell surface where *whorls* adjoin.

Teeth, cardinal The largest two or three teeth just under the *beak* of a clam.
Teeth, lateral Smaller, narrow and longer teeth in front or in back of the *cardinal teeth*.

Umbilicus A central cavity at the base of the shell, around which the *whorls* coil.
Umbo(Umbones) The *beak* or beginning part of a *bivalve*.
Univalve A mollusc shell having a single piece (a *gastropod*).

Valve One of the main shelly halves of a *bivalve*.
Varix An axial rib or swelling made during a major growth stoppage.

Whorl A turn or coil of a snail shell.

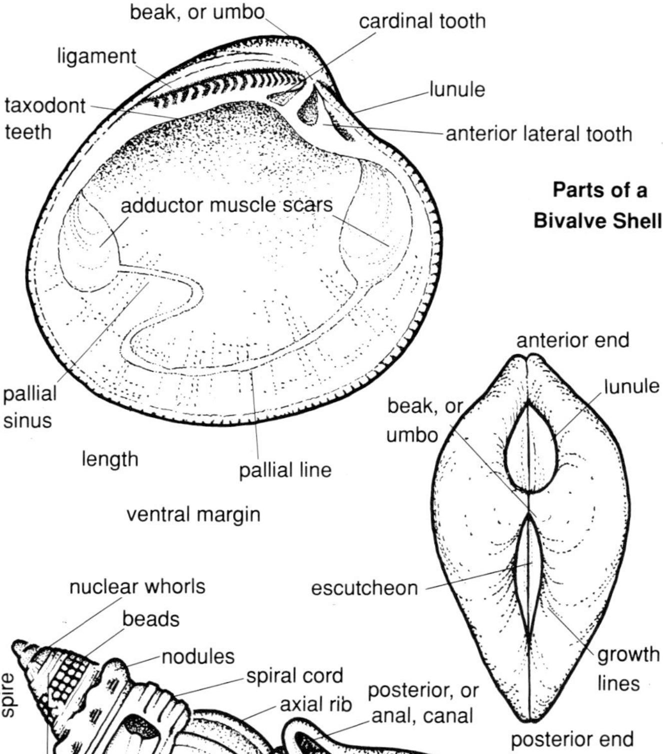

Parts of a Bivalve Shell

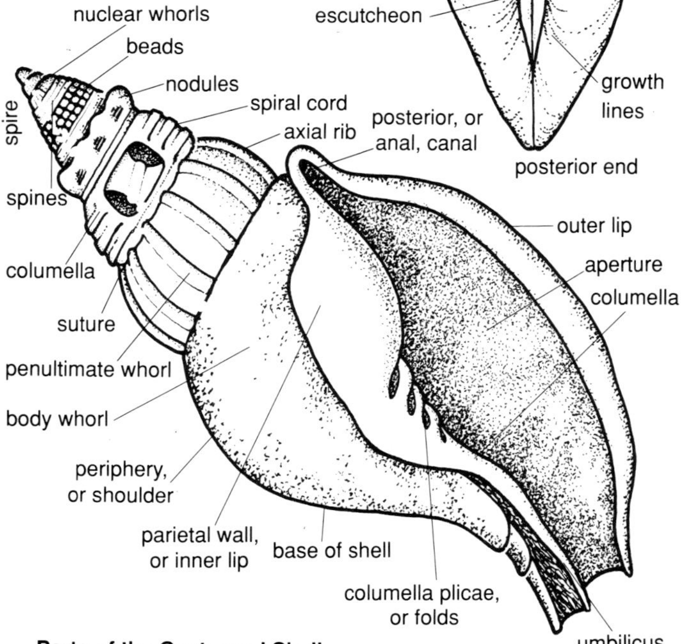

Parts of the Gastropod Shell

THE PRIMITIVE SNAILS

Abalones; Ormers
(*Family Haliotidae*)

Worldwide in distribution, the several dozen species of abalones, or ormers as they are called in Europe, are a popular food. The low shell with a large expanded last whorl is characterized by a vivid, iridescent, mother-of-pearl interior and by a series of small, round open holes that help in water circulation. All species live on rocks where encrusting algae are their main source of food.

Black Abalone, *Haliotis cracherodii* Leach, 1814. Shape usually oval, fairly deep, with a smooth outer surface, except for coarse growth lines. Exterior bluish to greenish black. Interior pearly white. About eight or nine holes open, but rarely in freaks they may be absent. This species is uncommon in Oregon, but more common in California where it occurs in crevices in intertidal rocks. The legal capture size is 5 in (12 cm) or more.

Black Abalone
6 in (15 cm)

Red Abalone, *Haliotis rufescens* Swainson, 1822. Oval, rather flattened. Outer surface rough, dull brick-red with a narrow red border around the inner edge of the shell. Interior bright, iridescent blue and greens, with a large central muscle scar. Usually only three or four holes are open. Its main range is from Oregon to central California.

Red Abalone
10 in (26 cm)

Northern Green Abalone, *Haliotis walallensis* Stearns, 1899. Oval-elongate, flattened, with numerous, small spiral threads. Exterior dark, brick-red, mottled with pale green. Moderately common from British Columbia to northern California.

Northern Green Abalone
5 in (12.5 cm)

Japanese Abalone, *Haliotis kamtschatkana* Jonas, 1845. Elongate, with a moderately high spire. Usually four or five holes open which have raised edges. Exterior of shell roughly corrugated, but a few specimens may have weak, spiral threads or cords. The soft parts are mottled tan and greenish, but some are tinged with orange. Tentacles green and slender. Moderately common in its northern range which is from Oregon to southern Alaska and Japan. Lives on subtidal rocks.

Japanese Abalone
4 in (10 cm)

European Ormer, *Haliotis tuberculata* Linnaeus, 1758. Shell elongate, with three or four rapidly expanding whorls. Exterior somewhat rough, with growth lines and fine spiral threads. Dark reddish brown or mottled in green. About nine or ten holes open. Interior bright, whitish, iridescent. Tentacles on head are long; eyes bluish. Uncommon on intertidal rocks in the Channel Islands, but commoner further south to the Mediterranean in 3 to 160 ft (1–50 m). A popular, edible species.

European Ormer
2.5 in (6.5 cm)

Crass Emarginula, *Emarginula crassa* Sowerby, 1813, is one of several, small slit limpets belonging to the family Fissurellidae that live on subtidal rocks throughout the temperate regions. The small white shells are coiled in their young stages, but grow into shield-shaped limpets. The narrow slit on the back edge of the shell serves as an exodus for water and waste products. This one-inch, white species is distributed from Norway and Iceland to Ireland and Scotland. Sculpture of fine reticulations and with about fifty fine, radiating threads. Fairly common, especially in the north, under stones in subtidal regions to depths of 655 ft (200 m).

Crass Emarginula
1 in (2.5 cm)

✦

Puncturellas
and Keyhole Limpets
(*Family Fissurellidae*)

These small, usually white limpets have a slot-like opening just in back of the hooked apex. Within the slot is a cup-like shelf. There are about sixty worldwide, mainly deepwater species. Most are believed to feed on sponges.

Hooded Puncturella, *Puncturella cucullata* (Gould, 1846) is a strong, fairly high shell with a small, elevated apex which is hooked over towards the front end. Behind it is a small, elongate slit penetrating through the shell. Exterior of shell with fourteen to twenty-three major radiating ribs with one to five smaller ones between. Fairly common from low

Hooded Puncturella
1 in (2.5 cm)

tide mark to 655 ft (200 m) from Alaska to northern California.

Helmet Puncturella, *Puncturella galeata* (Gould, 1846). Shell solid, fairly high, oval in outline with the larger, posterior half being slightly wider. Slit short and narrow. Ribs numerous, small and of irregular strengths. Exterior grey to whitish; interior glossy white. Lives in rocky and muddy areas from 100 to 490 ft (30–150 m). Moderately common from the Aleutian Islands to northern California coast.

Helmet Puncturella
0.7 in (2 cm)

Volcano Limpet, *Fissurella volcano* Reeve, 1849. Elongate-oval, fairly high shell with a single, oblong hole at the central apex. Sculpture of numerous, rather large, but low and rounded, radial ribs of varying sizes. Exterior grey, with pinkish mauve, radial rays. Interior glossy-white, with a pink line around the callus surrounding the hole. Common on intertidal rocky rubble; uncommon in Oregon, but more common further south to California.

Volcano Limpet
1 in (2.5 cm)

Cloudy Keyhole Limpet, *Fissurella nubecula* (Linnaeus, 1758). Ovate-elongate, fairly high and solid. Exterior with numerous, unequal radial riblets; grey with a dozen rays of dull-purple. Keyhole oblong, parallel-sided. Interior white and green-tinted. The internal callus around the keyhole is white or green and bounded by a brown line. A southern Mediterranean species living as far north as Portugal and southern France. Fairly common on subtidal rocks where it feeds on minute algae.

Cloudy Keyhole Limpet
1 in (2.5 cm)

Graecian Keyhole Limpet, *Diodora graeca* (Linnaeus, 1758). Shell oval, a little narrower in front. Keyhole is small, oval and located nearer the front end. Exterior with numerous, elevated, radiating ribs, alternately larger and smaller, with concentric thread intersecting to form small square pits. Colour dull yellow-brown, sometimes rayed with darker brown. Interior white, its margin strongly denticulate. Callus around the keyhole is squared off and minutely excavated behind. Feeds on sponges. Moderately common subtidally to 820 ft (250 m) on rocks. Southern coasts of the British Isles to the Mediterranean.

Graecian Keyhole Limpet
0.8 in (2.2 cm)

Italian Keyhole Limpet, *Diodora italica* (Defrance, 1820). Shell ovate, narrower in front, rather depressed; sides are slightly convex near the edge of the shell, but concave or straight near the small keyhole opening. Exterior with numerous, slightly rounded radial riblets of unequal size, crossed by very fine, concentric threads. Colour greyish yellow or solid grey; sometimes with darker purplish rays. Moderately common from Portugal to the Mediterranean on subtidal rocks.

Italian Keyhole Limpet
1.5 in (4 cm)

Rough Keyhole Limpet, *Diodora aspera* (Rathke, 1833). Shell ovate, slightly narrower in the front; moderately elevated. The flat-sided keyhole is almost round and located slightly towards the front. Exterior of rough, radial and numerous, weaker concentric threads. Colour greyish white with about twelve to eighteen irregularly sized, purplish blue radial colour bands. Interior bluish white; callus around the keyhole is truncated at the front end. It is commonly found attached to rocks from the low tide mark to several feet in depth. Ranges from Cook's Inlet, Alaska, southward to southern California.

Rough Keyhole Limpet
1.5 in (4 cm)

Two-spotted Keyhole Limpet, *Megatebennus bimaculatus* (Dall, 1871). Elongate-oblong, low, with the ends turned up slightly. Large apical keyhole is elongate-oblong, located at the centre of the shell. Numerous radial and concentric threads give the exterior a cancellate sculpturing. Brownish to grey with a wide, darker ray on each side. Interior glossy-white. Ranges from Alaska to southern California; common.

Two-spotted Keyhole Limpet
0.7 in (2 cm)

Blue-rayed Limpet, *Helcion pellucidum* (Linnaeus, 1758). Belonging to the following family, Patellidae, this common European species lives on the kelp weed, *Laminaria*. Cap-shaped, sometimes elevated, and has no keyhole or marginal slit. Surface smooth, shiny, horn-coloured with narrow, bright-blue rays. No operculum present. The white body has a large head with two tentacles, each bearing an eye at the base. Mantle edge with minute tentacles. This species breeds in winter and in the spring the planktonic young settle on fucoid seaweeds, and later move to kelp. Common subtidally from Norway to Portugal.

Blue-rayed Limpet
0.5 in (1.2 cm)

True Limpets
(Family Patellidae)

Several unrelated families produce limpet-shaped shells, but the true limpets are represented by the common, rock-dwelling genus *Patella* in Europe and South Africa. They differ from the similar-looking Acmaeidae of the Americas in lacking leaf-like gill plumes and in having only a gill cordon. No operculum present. Patellids are usually shallow-water rock-dwellers whose shells are greatly influenced by the environment. They are very common in Western Europe but absent in the cooler waters of North America.

Common European Limpet, *Patella vulgata* Linnaeus, 1758. Shell solid, oval and raised; exterior with numerous, irregular small riblets, between which may be smaller radial threads. Growth lines sometimes evident. Colour varying from whitish to yellowish, and rarely streaked with dark-brown. Interior weakly iridescent, the centre clouded with a whitish callus. A common, edible, rock-dwelling species living from Norway to the Mediterranean.

Limpets that live in the upper tidal region are usually higher in outline than those living closer to the constant impact of incoming waves.

Low and high form of Common European Limpet
2 in (5 cm)

European China Limpet, *Patella aspera* Röding, 1798. Similar to the Common European Limpet, but more elongate. Exterior with strong, sharper ribs, resulting in a serrated edge to the shell. Interior porcellaneous white, with a head scar of pale-orange. Common from the southern British Isles to southern France.

Common China Limpet
1.5 in (4 cm)

✦

American Limpets

(*Families Acmaeidae and Lottiidae*)

The western coast of North America abounds with a variety of limpets, many formerly placed in the genus *Collisella* (now *Lottia*). The family Acmaeidae includes the single, white-shelled limpet of the Pacific coast of North America and a few blind, small deep-sea pectinodont limpets. The remaining nineteen species of *Lottia* and *Tectura* belong to the family Lottiidae.

White-cap Limpet, *Acmaea mitra* Rathke, 1833. Shell white or greyish white, solid, conic in shape with an almost circular base. Apex pointed and near the centre. Often covered with small knobby millepore growths. Interior white. Edge of shell smooth. Rarely pink-rayed. Most abundant in its northern range from the Aleutian Islands, but uncommon as far south as southern California.

White-cap Limpet
1 in (2.5 cm)

Shield Limpet, *Lottia pelta* (Rathke, 1833). Shell strong, base elliptical in outline, with a moderately high apex situated almost near the centre. Exterior has about twenty-five very weak, radial riblets. Colour cream-grey with strong black radial, often intertwining, stripes. Inner border edge with alternating black and cream bars. A common intertidal rock-dweller from Alaska to Mexico.

Shield Limpet
1.2 in (3 cm)

File Limpet, *Lottia limatula* (Carpenter 1864). Base elliptical to almost round; low to quite flat. Characterized by radial rows of small beads which form tiny riblets. Exterior greenish black. Interior glossy white with bluish tint. Edge of shell usually has a solid, black-brown, narrow colour band. A common intertidal, rock species occurring from Puget Sound, Washington, south to southern California.

File Limpet
1.2 in (3 cm)

Fingered Limpet, *Lottia digitalis* (Rathke, 1833). Elliptical to ovate in outline; with a moderately high apex minutely hooked forward and placed one third back from the front edge. With fifteen to twenty-five moderately well-developed, coarse radial ribs which give the shell a wavy border. Colour greyish with tiny, distinct mottlings of white dots and blackish streaks and lines. Interior white with a faint bluish tint and with a large, usually even, head patch of dark-brown in the centre. Inner edge of shell with a solid or broken, narrow band of black-brown. A common species preferring vertical rock surfaces where action is severe. A homing species ranging from the Aleutians to California.

Fingered Limpet
1 in (2.5 cm)

Unstable Limpet, *Lottia instabilis* (Gould, 1846). A small, solid, all-brown species living on the stems of large kelp weeds. Shell heavy, oblong, with a high spire, and with its sides compressed. Lower edge curved so that the shell may fit evenly against its kelp stem substrate. Exterior smoothish, a dull light-brown. Interior whitish with a faint brown stain in the centre and with a narrow, solid border of brown. Moderately common from Alaska to southern California.

Unstable Limpet
1 in (2.5 cm)

Mask Limpet, *Tectura persona* (Rathke, 1833). Oval-elongate, smoothish, with a fairly high apex pointing forward and one third the way back from the front edge. Exterior smoothish with a fine pattern of white squares and triangles on a dark-grey background. Interior bluish white to blackish blue. This species is very common from northern California to Alaska where it lives between tides on rocks where strong waves flush the shaded rock crevices.

Mask Limpet
1.2 in (3 cm)

Pacific Plate Limpet, *Tectura scutum* (Rathke, 1833). Shell fairly large, almost round in outline, quite flat, with the apex towards the centre of the shell. Smoothish, except for very fine radial riblets, seen best in young specimens. Exterior greenish grey, with slate-grey radial bands or mottlings. Interior bluish white with faint or darkish brown head scar. Inner edge with alternating, small bars of blackish brown and bluish white. A rock-dweller along the coasts of Alaska to Oregon where it is common; in California it is rare.

A similar species, *Tectura tessulata* (Müller, 1776) from the British Isles is only 0.5 in (15 mm) narrower at the front end and has chocolate-brown radial patterns. It is locally called the Tortoiseshell Limpet and is common in rocky tidepools.

Pacific Plate Limpet
1.5 in (4 cm)

Rough Pacific Limpet, *Tectura scabra* (Gould, 1846). Elliptical in outline, with a fairly low apex located one third back from the front end. The fifteen to twenty-five strong, coarse radiating ribs make the edge wavy. Colour a dirty grey-green. Interior glossy, whitish and irregularly stained in the centre with brown. Edge of the shell between the serrations stained with purplish brown. A common species found clinging to gently sloping rock surfaces. It is a southern species ranging from Oregon to Baja California.

Rough Pacific Limpet
1 in (2.5 cm)

Seaweed Limpet, *Discurria insessa* (Hinds, 1842). A small, solid shell, with a high spire and compressed, parallel sides. Twice as long as wide. Exterior a uniform, greasy light-brown. Abundant on the stalks and holdfasts of the large kelps, such as *Egregia*. Occurs along the Pacific coast from Alaska to Baja California.

Seaweed Limpet
0.6 in (1.5 cm)

✦

Trochoid Snails
(*Family Trochidae*)

This is a very diversified snail family, of many genera and species, found in most parts of the world, from intertidal habitats to very deep water. Most have an iridescent, mother-of-pearl finish inside the top-shaped shell. The operculum is circular, of many whorls and corneous.

Greenland Margarite, *Margarites groenlandicus* (Gmelin, 1791). Shell small, trochoid in shape, with the angle of the spire about 110°. Whorls strongly rounded, aperture round, umbilicus wide and deep. Outer lip and columella very thin. Base smooth; top of whorls glassy-smooth. Suture is finely impressed. Colour glossy-cream. Common on sandy and rock bottoms from 30 to 985 ft (10–300 m) from the Arctic Seas to Maine and to the British Isles.

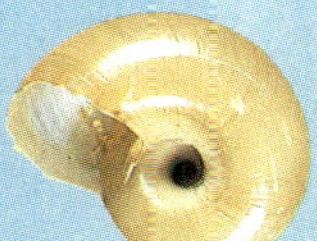

Greenland Margarite
0.5 in (1.2 cm)

Northern Rosy Margarite, *Margarites costalis* (Gould, 1841). Shell a little wider than high and with five evenly and well-rounded whorls. Narrowly and deeply umbilicate. Angle of spire about 90°. Next to last whorl with two to four unequal, raised spiral cords. Base with eight to ten threads. Colour rosy to greyish cream. White within the smooth umbilicus. Aperture pearly-rose. Common from Greenland to Massachusetts; and from Alaska.

Northern Rosy Margarite
0.5 in (1.2 cm)

Sordid Margarite, *Margarites sordidus* (Hancock, 1846). Shell very similar to *M. costalis*, but usually larger, with more rounded whorls, finer spiral, uneven threads, and with numerous, very fine, slanting, axial threads. Suture more strongly indented, below which are crowded, short, slanting riblets. This species is found in Arctic waters around the world.

Sordid Margarite
0.8 in (2 cm)

Puppet Margarite, *Margarites pupillus* (Gould, 1849). Trochoid in shape. Five or six whorls, the upper ones with five or six smoothish, small, spiral threads between or over which are microscopic, axial, slanting threads. Umbilicus narrow and deep. Exterior a dull, chalky-white to yellowish grey. Aperture rosy to greenish pearl. A common littoral species from Alaska to Oregon.

Puppet Margarite
0.4 in (1 cm)

Lovely Pacific Solarelle, *Solariella permabilis* Carpenter, 1864. Shell small, as long as wide, solid, semi-glossy. Umbilicus fairly wide, round, very deep and bordered by a strong beaded cord. Seven whorls, shouldered just below the suture by a flat shelf. Colour tan with light-mauve streaks and mottlings. Moderately common on rocky rubble bottoms from 330 to 1970 ft (100–600 m). Japan and Alaska south to off California.

Lovely Pacific Solarelle
0.7 in (2 cm)

Obscure Solarelle, *Solariella obscura* (Couthouy, 1838). Shell small; whorls strongly shouldered by one or two large, feebly beaded, spiral cords above the periphery. Base smoothish, except for microscopic spiral scratches. Umbilicus narrow and bordered by an angular rim. Colour greyish to pinkish tan, often eroded to reveal a pearly-golden colour. Commonly dredged from 20 to 2,600 ft (6–800 m) from the Arctic Seas to Virginia and from Alaska to Washington; also Norway.

Obscure Solarelle
0.4 in (1 cm)

Otto's Spiny Margarite, *Lischkeia ottoi* (Philippi, 1844). Shell small, lightweight, as wide as long. Exterior pearly-white. Sculpture of whorls in the spire with three evenly spaced, spiral rows of prickly beads. Nuclear whorls with axial riblets. Nova Scotia to off North Carolina and from Norway to off France.

Otto's Spiny Margarite
0.7 in (2 cm)

Regular Spiny Margarite, *Lischkeia regularis* (Verrill and Smith, 1880). Similar to *L. ottoi*, but the umbilicus is nearly closed, the whorls are more rounded and well-beaded by three or four prominent spiral rows of tiny, sharp beads. The base has five spiral threads bearing minute

Regular Spiny Margarite
0.7 in (2 cm)

beads. Colour greyish, dull-white. Fairly common offshore from Nova Scotia to off New York.

Adams' Spiny Margarite, *Lischkeia cidaris* (Carpenter, 1864). Shell moderately fragile, sculptured with three or four spiral rows of fairly large beads. Suture deeply indented. Base with seven or eight smaller, weakly beaded, spiral cords. Outer lip thin and wavy. Exterior greyish tan. Operculum thin, translucent brown, multispiral. Moderately common offshore from Alaska to southern California.

Adams' Spiny Margarite
1.5 in (4 cm)

Northern Top-shell, *Calliostoma occidentale* (Mighels and Adams, 1842). Shell small, trochoid, glistening iridescent white. Whorls convex and with three or four strong spiral cords, the lower ones smooth, the uppermost neatly beaded. No umbilicus. Outer lip fragile, slightly crenulated. Interior pearly white. Spire straight-sided, sometimes with a reddish tinge. Common from Nova Scotia to off New Jersey; Scandinavia and Iceland to northern British Isles.

Northern Top-shell
0.5 in (1.2 cm)

Baird's Top-shell, *Calliostoma bairdii* Verrill and Smith, 1880. Shell solid, with straight sides and an apical angle of about 70°. Base rather flat, periphery of the last whorl strongly angular. Sculpture of six or seven spiral rows of small, neat beads. No umbilicus. Colour brownish cream with faint maculations of iridescent reddish. Moderately common offshore from New England to northeastern Florida.

Baird's Top-shell
1 in (2.5 cm)

Ringed Top-shell, *Calliostoma annulatum* (Lightfoot, 1786). An unusually beautiful shell, trochoid in shape, with a flattish spire at an angle of about 70°. Lightweight, golden-yellow in background colour with a mauve band at the periphery of the whorls. Has numerous spiral rows of tiny, distinct beads, usually five to eight rows in the spire whorls. Nucleus pink. No umbilicus. Outer lip sharp and finely crenulated. Operculum corneous, circular and light-yellow. Ranges from southern Alaska to northern Baja California.

Ringed Top-shell
1 in (2.5 cm)

Channeled Top-shell, *Calliostoma canaliculatum* (Lightfoot, 1786). Shell lightweight, spire sharp and with straight sides. Periphery of last whorl rather sharp and angular. Base of shell almost flat. The numerous sharp spiral cords are slightly beaded and make the suture between whorls difficult to distinguish. Nuclear whorls white. Fairly common on kelps. Ranges from Alaska to southern California.

Channeled Top-shell
1.5 in (4 cm)

Western Ribbed Top-shell, *Calliostoma ligatum* (Gould, 1849). Shell solid and rather heavy, with well-rounded whorls. Six to eight strong, smooth spiral, light-brown cords on a background of dark-chocolate. Rarely flushed with mauve. No umbilicus. Aperture pearly white. A very common littoral species from Alaska to northern California, but rare southward.

Western Ribbed Top-shell
0.8 in (2 cm)

Variable Top-shell, *Calliostoma variegatum* (Carpenter, 1864). Shell solid, its spire slightly concave and the indented sutures quite prominent. Periphery of the last whorl well-rounded. Five or six beaded cords on the above whorls. Nucleus pinkish. Colour light-tan with speckles of reddish brown. Ranges from Alaska to southern California.

Variable Top-shell
1 in (2.5 cm)

European Painted Top-shell, *Calliostoma zizyphinus* Linnaeus, 1758. Solid, trochoid in shape, with a flat-sided apex with an angle of about 70°. Periphery on last whorl well-rounded. Whorls with three to five spiral, smooth cords, the largest being just above the suture. Colour pale-yellow with streaks and blotches of darker tan. Umbilicus slightly.indented. Ranges from Norway to the Mediterranean.

European Painted Top-shell
1 in (2.5 cm)

European Granular Top-shell, *Calliostoma granulatum* (Born, 1778). Spire pointed, slightly concave. Whorls above have six or seven smaller, beaded spiral threads. Suture minutely indented. Base of shell with a dozen faint spiral threads and coloured cream with numerous reddish brown spots. Uncommon from 23 to 985 ft (7–300 m) on rough, stony bottoms. Ranges from the southern British Isles to the Azores and Mediterranean.

European Granular Top-shell
1 in (2.5 cm)

Gualteri's Top-shell, *Calliostoma gualterianum* (Philippi, 1848). Shell conical-elevated, without an umbilicus, polished, solid, yellowish brown or olive, clouded with dark-brown, the earlier whorls bluish black. Colours variable, and rarely all purple. A common shallow-water species ranging from Portugal, south into the Mediterranean.

Gualteri's Top-shell
0.5 in (1.2 cm)

Exasperating Top-shell, *Jujubinus exasperatus* (Pennant, 1777). Shell small, solid, pyramidal with a high spire and flat sides. Sculpture of three or four large, rounded, coarsely beaded cords. Base with six flattish, smooth cords. Umbilicus absent. Colour of variable maculations of reds, browns and tans. Fairly common from southern England south into the Mediterranean.

Exasperating Top-shell
0.4 in (10 cm)

Black Tegula, *Tegula funebralis* (A. Adams, 1855). Heavy, solid, dark purple-black in colour; smoothish, but with a narrow, puckered band just below the suture. Weak spiral cords rarely evident; coarse growth lines present in large, more elongate specimens. Base rounded. Umbilicus closed or merely a slight dimple. Columella pearly, with two small nodules at the base. The head and tentacles are entirely black. The sole of the foot of males is usually light-cream in colour, that of the females usually brownish. A very common littoral, rock-dwelling species ranging from Vancouver, Canada, to southern California.

Black Tegula
1.5 in (4 cm)

Magical Gibbula, *Gibbula magus* (Linnaeus, 1758). Shell solid, low-spired, with shouldered whorls bearing coarse nodules just below the suture. Last whorl keeled and smooth. Umbilicus small. Base with fine spiral lines. Last whorl with irregular, slanting axial swellings. Columella thin, white, with a bulge in the centre. Colour variable browns and reddish maculations. Animal yellowish pink with blackish purple blotches. A subtidal species in southern British Isles and south into the Mediterranean.

Magical Gibbula
2 in (3 cm)

Ashen Gibbula, *Gibbula cineraria* (Linnaeus, 1758). Shell solid, somewhat dome-shaped with a slightly convex spire and blunt apex. Sculpture of numerous, low, slightly nodulose, spiral ridges crossed by fine growth lines. Umbilicus narrow but deep. Colour yellowish with numerous broken, slanting streaks of brownish purple. A very common intertidal species on rocky shores among weeds and under stones. Found throughout the British Isles and from Iceland to Portugal.

Ashen Gibbula
0.8 in (2 cm)

Umbilicate Gibbula, *Gibbula umbilicalis* (da Costa, 1778). Shell solid, somewhat globular, with a convex, rounded spire and flat apex. Surface smoothish, except for fine, incised lines and eight to ten grooves on the base. Umbilicus fairly large and deep. Colour heavily maculated with speckles of reddish brown on a cream background; sometimes with axial, slanting flames of red-brown. A common intertidal species found among weeds and stones in tidepools. Eggs are laid singly and fertilized externally by floating

Umbilicate Gibbula
0.8 in (2 cm)

sperm. Ranges from the southern British Isles to the Mediterranean.

Lined Monodont, *Monodonta lineata* (da Costa, 1778). Shell globose, large, heavy, with somewhat rounded whorls. Surface smoothish to rough with low, weak, spiral ridges. Irregular growth lines are frequent. Colour dark-grey with a fine mottled pattern and a large white area surrounding the indented umbilical area. Columella with a swollen, small tooth near the base. The animal is greyish green with numerous black lines. A fairly common rock pool-dweller, feeding on vegetable detritus and soft algae. Ranges from the southern British Isles to Portugal.

Lined Monodont
1.2 in (3 cm)

Articulate Monodont, *Monodonta articulata* Lamarck, 1822. Shell solid, trochoid in shape, with a rounded spire. Umbilicus absent. Surface rough. Colour grey-green or dirty white, with numerous spiral bands of alternating squares of white and reddish brown. Some specimens are conspicuously spirally grooved, some quite smooth. A common southern littoral snail ranging from southern France and Portugal to the Mediterranean.

Articulate Monodont
1 in (2.5 cm)

THE ADVANCED SHELLS

Periwinkles
(*Family Littorinidae*)

Throughout most parts of the world the small periwinkles appear in large numbers along rocky shores between tide marks or on wharf pilings and mangrove trees. They feed on vegetable detritus and living algae.

Common Periwinkle, *Littorina littorea* (Linnaeus, 1758). Shell globular, solid, with a coarse exterior and a strong, thin outer lip. Columella arched, smooth and white. Sculpture of faint spiral lines. Colour drab greyish, sometimes with fine, spiral streaks of whitish. This species is common on intertidal rocks in exposed areas. It ranges from Greenland and Norway to the Mediterranean; and from northern Canada to Delaware.

Common Periwinkle
1 in (2.5 cm)

Marsh Periwinkle, *Littorina irrorata* (Say, 1822). Thick-shelled, with numerous, regularly formed, spiral grooves. Outer lip slightly flaring and with tiny grooves on the inside. Colour greyish, with tiny, short streaks of reddish brown on the spiral ridges. Aperture yellowish. Columella reddish brown. Commonly found in large numbers among the sedges of brackish water marshes. Ranges from New York to central Florida and to Texas.

Marsh Periwinkle
1 in (2.5 cm)

Northern Yellow Periwinkle, *Littorina obtusata* (Linnaeus, 1758). Small, globular, solid, with a low spire and smoothish exterior. Colour variable but usually a uniform bright brownish yellow or orange-yellow. Operculum yellowish or brownish. It is a common rocky coast species, found from southern Labrador to New Jersey; Norway to the Mediterranean.

Northern Yellow Periwinkle
0.5 in (1.2 cm)

Northern Rough Periwinkle, *Littorina saxatilis* (Olivi, 1792). Shell solid, with a pointed spire, rather distinctly rounded whorls and an impressed suture. Surface smoothish, except for numerous, indistinct spiral threads which are usually sharply sloping in cross-section. Typical form grey with a darker tessellate pattern and a dark aperture. The form (or another species) *rudis* Maton, 1797, lacks the tessellate pattern, has a broader lower columella and the aperture is light-coloured. A moderately common, high intertidal, rock species. It lives in the Arctic Seas south to New Jersey; south to Puget Sound, Washington; and south from Norway to France.

Northern Rough Periwinkle
0.5 in (1.2 cm)

Eroded Periwinkle, *Littorina keenae* Rosewater, 1978. Shell small, with a pointed spire, usually badly eroded. Colour greyish brown with bluish white spots and flecks. There is a flattened, eroded area on the body whorl alongside the whitish columella. Interior of aperture chocolate-brown with a white spiral band at the bottom. An abundant species on rocky

Eroded Periwinkle
0.7 in (2 cm)

shore flats in the splash zone. Found from Puget Sound, Washington, to Mexico. Formerly called *Littorina planaxis* Philippi.

Checkered Periwinkle, *Littorina scutulata* Gould, 1849. Shell small, somewhat elongate, with a pointed spire. The columella is not as broad as that in the Eroded Periwinkle. Surface smooth, semi-glossy. Colour light to dark reddish brown, and often with fairly large, irregular spots and blotches of bluish white. Common in the upper intertidal zone. Distributed from Kodiak Island, Alaska, south to the northwestern part of Baja California, Mexico.

Checkered Periwinkle
0.5 in (1.2 cm)

✦

Purple Sea-snails and Turret-shells

(Families Janthinidae and Turritellidae)

The purple sea-snails are a small family of pelagic snails, usually inhabiting the surface of warm seas, but sometimes drifting into colder waters. A float of bubbles is created by the animal, and in some species the egg capsules are attached to the underside. The elongate, narrow, many-whorled turret-shells are mostly warm-water, mud-dwellers with only a few species occurring in cold waters. The operculum is thin, chitinous, circular, with many whorls and often has bristles along the edge.

Common Purple Sea-snail, *Janthina janthina* (Linnaeus, 1758). Whorls angular, two-toned with purplish white on the apex side and deep violet on the umbilical side. Base of columella not extended. Rarely cast ashore in southern New England and the British Isles.

Common Purple Sea-snail
1 in (2.5 cm)

Eroded Turret-shell, *Tachyrhynchus erosus* (Couthouy, 1838). Elongate, eight to ten whorls which have five or six flat-topped, spiral cords. No umbilicus. Aperture round; columella smooth. Colour chalky-cream with a polished, tan periostracum. Common from 45 to 460 ft (14–140 m) on mud bottoms. Arctic Seas to off Massachusetts and also south to British Columbia.

Eroded Turret-shell
1 in (2.5 cm)

Common Turret-shell, *Turritella communis* Risso, 1829. Elongate, about fifteen whorls; spire usually eroded. Spiral cords small and numerous. Brownish yellow with the base tinged with lilac. Abundant in muddy, shallow waters from Norway to North Africa.

Common Turret-shell
1 in (2.5 cm)

Wentletraps
(*Family Epitoniidae*)

The wentletraps are a popular group of shells noted for their pure-white shells bearing numerous, sharp, axial ribs. The aperture is always round and fitted with a black or brown, chitinous operculum. The white animal feeds on sea-anemones and when disturbed may give off a purple fluid. The family has numerous genera, with shells that are smooth, reticulated or with sharp ribs.

Northern White Wentletrap
1 in (2.5 cm)

Northern White Wentletrap, *Acirsa borealis* (Lyell, 1842). Elongate, chalky-white to yellowish; surface has very weak, axial riblets, and numerous, spiral cut lines, sometimes filled with thin periostracum. Two nuclear whorls are smooth. Edge of outer lip thin. Uncommon from just offshore down to 330 ft (100 m). Aleutian Islands to Greenland and south to Massachusetts.

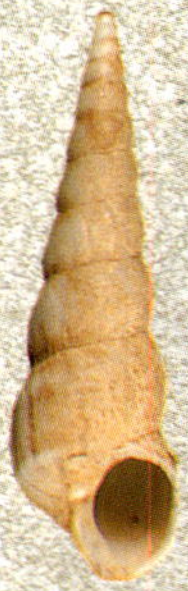

Costate Wentletrap
1.2 in (3 cm)

Costate Wentletrap, *Acirsa costulata* (Mighels and Adams, 1842) is very similar to *A. borealis* and is sometimes considered a synonym. It is much more elongate, the spire angle is much less, the base of the whorls have a weak carina, the surface is smoother and yellowish. Uncommon offshore in New England waters.

Wroblewski's Wentletrap, *Opalia wroblewskii* (Mörch, 1876).

Elongate, solid, always looks beachworn. Greyish white, but often stained purple from its own dye. Has six to eight low, pronounced axial ribs. Base of shell bounded by a strong, smooth, low spiral cord. Fairly common from 3 to 330 ft (1–100 m) from Alaska to southern California.

Wroblewski's Wentletrap
1 in (2.5 cm)

Money Wentletrap, *Epitonium indianorum* (Carpenter, 1864). Slender, with about ten well-rounded whorls and a deeply indented suture. Each whorl has fourteen or fifteen sharp, axial ribs which are slightly bent backwards. Tops of the ribs are slightly pointed. Fairly common offshore on gravel bottoms associated with sea-anemones. In shallow water from Alaska to British Columbia, but in deeper water further south to Baja California and Mexico.

Money Wentletrap
1 in (2.5 cm)

Greenland Wentletrap, *Epitonium greenlandicum* (Perry, 1811). Solid, elongate, chalky-grey, with nine to twelve ridge-like, sometimes broad, ribs per whorl. Spiral sculpture prominent, with nine spiral cords on base of shell. Operculum dark-brown. Common offshore on gravel bottoms from 65 to 850 ft (20–260 m). Ranges from Alaska to British Columbia and from Greenland to Long Island, New York.

Greenland Wentletrap
1.2 in (3 cm)

Angulate Wentletrap, *Epitonium angulatum* (Say, 1830). Moderately stout, strong and pure-white. Eight whorls with about nine or ten strong, but thin, axial ribs which are very slightly reflected backwards and which are usually angulated at the shoulder. The ribs are usually lined up one below the other. Outer lip thickened and reflected. One of the commonest shallow-water, sand-dwelling wentletraps ranging from New York to Florida and to Texas.

Angulate Wentletrap
1 in (2.5 cm)

Humphrey's Wentletrap, *Epitonium humphreysi* (Kiener, 1838). Fairly slender, thick-shelled, dull-white and with a deep suture. The nine or ten convex whorls each have eight or nine ribs that are slightly angled at the shoulder. Outer lip round and thickened. Common from sandy shores to 330 ft (100 m). Extends from Massachusetts to Florida and to Texas.

Humphrey's Wentletrap
0.8 in (2 cm)

Brown-banded Wentletrap, *Epitonium rupicola* (Kurtz, 1860). Moderately stout, whitish to yellowish with two brownish spiral bands on either side of the deep suture. Twelve to eighteen weak or strong riblets on each whorl. A former, thickened varix is sometimes present on the whorl above. Base of shell has a single, fine spiral cord. Common from low water to about 130 ft (40 m). Ranges from Massachusetts to Florida and to Texas.

Brown-banded Wentletrap
1 in (2.5 cm)

Common European Wentletrap, *Epitonium clathrus* (Linnaeus, 1758). Elongate, strong; whorls barely meeting but linked and braced by eight or nine strong, axial ribs. Behind the thick, round outer lip there is a swollen varix. Colour greyish yellow; the ribs spotted with brown spiral lines. Animal white with purplish black specks. Common from intertidal sand flats to 230 ft (70 m). Norway to the Mediterranean and Black Sea.

Common European Wentletrap
1.5 in (4 cm)

Turton's Wentletrap, *Epitonium turtonis* (Turton, 1819). Similar to *E. clathrus*, but the whorls are more flat-sided, with twelve to fifteen ribs per whorl, the top of the ribs reflected and flattened against the sutures, and is usually more darkly coloured. Spaces between ribs with fine, spiral scratches. Moderately common on sandy bottoms from 16 to 65 ft (5–20 m). Ranges from Norway to Portugal.

Turton's Wentletrap
1.5 in (4 cm)

Trevely's Wentletrap, *Epitonium trevelyanum* (Johnston, 1841). Shell white, moderately elongate, with about fourteen ribs per whorl, the tops being thickened, triangular and flattened. Suture very deep. Spiral lines sometimes present, as well as a peripheral brown, spiral band. Uncommon offshore from Norway to Portugal.

Trevely's Wentletrap
0.8 in (2 cm)

✦

Hairy-shells

(*Family Trichotropidae*)

Members of this cold-water family are characterized by the hairy periostracal layer covering the outer shell. They have a turbinate shell with a short, pointed spire and a fairly large aperture. The operculum is chitinous, with few whorls. In some species, one-year-old snails are males, but turn into females in the second year, and die after laying their gelatinous egg capsules.

Two-keeled Hairy-shell, *Trichotropis bicarinata* (Sowerby, 1825). Shell as wide as tall, with a sharp apex, and about four whorls which have two strong, spiral cords at the periphery. The columella is wide and flattened. The delicate periostracum is brown and very spinose on the shoulders of the whorls. Moderately common offshore. Occurs in Arctic Seas to the Queen Charlotte Islands, British Columbia, and Labrador and Newfoundland.

Two-keeled Hairy-shell
1.5 in (4 cm)

Grey Hairy-shell, *Trichotropis insignis* Middendorff, 1849. Similar to *T. bicarinata* but less than 1 in (2 cm). A heavier shell, weakly carinate, with numerous, uneven spiral threads, and a thin greyish periostracum. Uncommon offshore from Alaska to northern Japan.

Grey Hairy-shell
1 in (2.5 cm)

Cancellate Hairy-shell, *Trichotropis borealis* (Hinds, 1843). Has five or six rounded whorls bearing between sutures four or five strong, spiral cords, between which there may be small, axial riblets which produce a cancellate sculpture. Spire high. Periostracum thick, brown and with bristles over the region of the cords. A common shallow-water species from the Bering Sea to off Oregon.

Cancellate Hairy-shell
0.8 in (2 cm)

Cap Limpets and Chinese Hats (*Families Capulidae and Crepidulidae*)

The cap limpets begin life as small, coiled shells, but upon settling on a stone or bivalve shell, they grow into a cap-shaped limpet. The proboscis, which is formed from the forefoot, is permanently extended from the mouth and used to gather food or the pseudofeces of its bivalve host.

The chinese hats, or cup-and-saucer shells, are related to the slipper shells but have an extra shelf or cup within the main shell. They lack an operculum and are ciliary feeders, trapping floating food particles on a mucous sheet on the gills.

Fool's Cap Limpet, *Capulus ungaricus* (Linnaeus, 1767). Cap-shaped, with a small hooked apex. Shell strong, yellowish white, with an ashy-brown, shaggy periostracum. Irregularly sculptured with coarse threads. Ranges from Greenland to off northeast Florida; and from Norway and Iceland to Portugal.

Fool's Cap Limpet
1.5 in (4 cm)

Pacific Chinese Hat, *Calyptraea fastigiata* Gould, 1856. Outline of the base of the thin, strong shell is circular and the apex is at the centre of the shell. Colour white to grey. Moderately common offshore, attached to other shells and to stones. Ranges from Alaska to California.

Pacific Chinese Hat
1 in (2.5 cm)

European Chinese Hat, *Calyptraea chinensis* (Linnaeus, 1758). Similar to the Pacific Chinese Hat; exterior with concentric, pustulose growth rings. Common subtidally on other shells and on stones. Ranges from the British Isles to Portugal.

European Chinese Hat
0.6 in (1.5 cm)

✦

Slipper-shells
(*Family Crepidulidae*)

The curious cup inside the cup-and-saucer shells and the broad shelf within the slipper-shells are for the protection of the soft digestive gland of the animal. Most species adhere permanently to other dead shells, with the smaller males usually attached to the larger females. Males customarily turn into females after the second or third year. Eggs, laid in soft capsules, are attached to the substrate under the shell and are brooded until the free-swimming larval stages emerge.

Striate Cup-and-saucer, *Crucibulum striatum* Say, 1824. Cap-shaped; base circular, with the slightly twisted, smooth apex near the centre of the shell. Interior shelly cap two-thirds free from attachment. Exterior grey, with small, wavy radial cords. Commonly dredged offshore from 20 to 650 ft (6–200 m). Found in the Maritime Provinces of Canada to off Florida.

Striate Cup-and-saucer
1 in (2.5 cm)

Pacific Half-slipper, *Crepipatella lingulata* (Gould, 1846). Shell small, with an almost circular base; apex near edge of shell. Interior tannish mauve with a small cup attached along one side only. Exterior wrinkled and brownish. Common on living snail shells. Ranges from the Bering Sea to Panama.

Pacific Half-slipper
0.7 in (2 cm)

Hooked Slipper-shell, *Crepidula adunca* Sowerby, 1825. Highly arched, with a sharp, hooked apex. Laterally compressed, giving a triangular appearance from the sides. Colour dark brown with lighter rays and spots. Interior brown. Commonly found on small shells. Ranges from British Columbia to southern California.

Hooked Slipper-shell
1 in (2.5 cm)

European White Slipper-shell, *Crepidula unguiformis* Lamarck, 1822. Shell pure-white, solid, usually quite flat, or concave if attached to the interior aperture of a large gastropod shell. Apex at the end and with small, glossy nuclear whorls. Inner shelf about half the length of the entire shell, glossy-white and slightly concave. Exterior dull-white to dirty-grey. Commonly found on large dead shells. This is a southern species ranging from southern France and Portugal to the Mediterranean.

European White Slipper-shell
1 in (2.5 cm)

Western White Slipper-shell, *Crepidula nummaria* Gould, 1846. Shell elongate, flattened and slightly concave, with a glossy-white underside and a large deck which usually has a weak, raised ridge running from the apical end forward to the leading edge of the shelf. Exterior whitish, usually with a thin, yellowish periostracum. Found in rock crevices and the apertures of dead shells. Extends along the entire west coast from Alaska to Panama, usually in shallow water.

Western white Slipper-shell
1.2 in (3 cm)

Eastern White Slipper-shell, *Crepidula plana* Say, 1822. Shell thin but strong; pure-white. Very flat, sometimes convex or concave depending upon the shape of the substrate. The glossy-white shelf is smooth and somewhat convex. The apex is rarely turned to one side. Several specimens customarily congregate on dead shells or horseshoe crabs, *Limulus*, with the larger ones being females and the smaller, surrounding ones being males. When the female dies or is removed, the nearest male gradually turns into a female. The egg capsules are brooded under the front of the foot of the female. Slipper-shells are diatom filter feeders. This very common species extends from eastern Canada to Texas and south to Brazil.

Eastern White Slipper-shell
1.2 in (3 cm)

Convex Slipper-shell, *Crepidula convexa* Say, 1822. Shell small, usually highly arched and coloured a dark reddish to purplish brown. Some specimens may be spotted. The edge of the deck is almost straight. There is a small muscle scar inside the main shell on the right side just under the outer corner of the deck. Most live on other dead shells, but sometimes they settle on eelgrass where specimens become long and narrow. Occurs from Massachusetts to Texas and the

Convex Slipper-shell
0.5 in (1.2 cm)

West Indies. Introduced to California prior to 1899.

Common Atlantic Slipper-shell, *Crepidula fornicata* (Linnaeus, 1758). Shelly deck extends over the rear half of the inside of the arched shell. The deck is usually slightly concave and white to buff; its edge is strongly sinuate or waved in two places. Exterior dirty-white to tan, sometimes with brown blotches and lines. Variable in shape. They may be strongly corrugated if living on a ribbed scallop. This common, shallow-water species has been introduced to northwestern America and western Europe. Its normal range is from the Maritime Provinces of Canada to Texas.

Common Atlantic Slipper-shell
1.5 in (4 cm)

White Hoof-shell, *Hipponix antiquatus* (Linnaeus, 1767). Small, heavy for its size, cap-shaped, with a poorly developed spire. Nuclear whorls minute, spiral and glossy-white. There is a horseshoe-shaped muscle scar inside the shell. Exterior with prominent, rugose ribs crossed by incised lines. Periostracum thin, light-yellow. Sometimes with strong, smooth, circular cords. No operculum. Belongs to the family Hipponicidae. Found intertidally under stones or on other shells from British Columbia to Peru; and from Florida to Brazil.

White Hoof-shell
0.5 in (1.2 cm)

Lamellaria and Velutina Snails
(*Families Lamellariidae and Velutinidae*)

The lamellarian snails have very thin, fragile shells that are buried in a large, slug-like animal. They are associated with shallow-water, compound ascidians upon which they feed and lay their eggs. They are hermaphroditic, with all individuals bearing a short, prong-like penis.

Transparent Lamellaria, *Lamellaria perspicua* (Linnaeus, 1758). Shell fragile, smooth, transparent, almost without growth lines, and with two whorls. Nuclear whorl is slightly elevated. Columella slit open, so apex can be seen from below. Operculum absent. Uncommon in rock pools down to 330 ft (100 m). Occurs from Norway and Iceland to the Mediterranean; eastern United States to Florida and to Brazil.

Transparent Lamellaria
0.5 in (1.2 cm)

Smooth Velutina, *Velutina velutina* (Müller, 1776). Shell very thin, fragile, translucent-amber, and covered with a thick, brownish periostracum which is spirally ridged. Columella arched and narrow. Found in the low tide area on rocky shores where it feeds on solitary ascidians. This is a circumboreal species extending south to the British Isles, California and to Massachusetts.

Smooth Velutina
0.7 in (1.7 cm)

False Arctic Slipper-shell, *Capulacmaea commodum* (Middendorff, 1851). A thin-shelled, white, cap-shaped shell covered with a thin brown periostracum. The shell is sometimes strongly rayed near the anterior end. This cold-water species is in the family Velutinidae, and has a wide distribution in circumpolar waters.

False Arctic Slipper-shell
1 in (2.5 cm)

✦

Pelican Foot Shells
(*Family Aporrhaidae*)

In what was once a widely distributed and diverse family of snails, less than a half-dozen now survive in the northern Atlantic. The outer lip of the shell is expanded into the shape of a webbed foot of a bird. They are detritus feeders that live on muddy bottoms. The foot is elongate and bears a long, narrow, chitinous operculum.

American Pelican's Foot, *Aporrhais occidentalis* Beck, 1836. Spire high, whorls well-rounded and with fifteen to twenty-five curved axial ribs per whorl. Numerous spiral threads present. Outer lip greatly flaring, its edge thickened and the top pointing upwards. Colour ashen-grey. Common from 33 to 1640 ft (10-500 m) in depth from Arctic Canada to off North Carolina.

American Pelican's Foot
2.3 in (6 cm)

Common Pelican's Foot, *Aporrhais pespelecani* (Linnaeus, 1758). Spire sharp, the whorls in the spire with about twelve axial, elongate knobs. On the last whorl there is a second row of rounded knobs. Outer lip expanded above and below, as well as having two or three extensions on the greatly expanded central part. Colour cream–tan. Lives partially buried in mud offshore. Abundant from Norway to the Mediterranean.

Common Pelican's Foot
1.2 in (3 cm)

MacAndrew's Pelican's Foot, *Aporrhais serresianus* (Michaud, 1828). Shell similar to the Common Pelican's Foot, but it is smaller, with thinner, longer, more delicate spines, and with weaker, more numerous axial ribs and knobs. *A. macandreae* Jeffreys, 1867, is a synonym. Deep water from the northern British Isles to Norway.

MacAndrew's Pelican's Foot
0.8 in (2 cm)

Trivias
(*Family Eratoidae*)

Known as members of the "allied cowries", these small, bright shells resemble the true tropical cowries in shape only. Most live in warm seas, but there are three exceptions in western Europe where some of them are popularly called "groats" or "nuns". They have a colourful mantle which extends up over the shell. There is no operculum. The trivias are shallow-water dwellers and feed upon compound ascidians.

Nun Trivia, *Trivia monacha* (da Costa, 1778). Shell globular, solid, with about twenty-eight strong, neat cords running over the rounded top surface. Aperture narrow, with about sixteen small teeth on the concave columellar side. Colour brownish pink with three diffused, darker spots on the top. Moderately common under stones and within rock crevices at the low tide mark. Ranges from the British Isles to the Mediterranean.

Nun Trivia
0.8 in (2 cm)

Arctic Trivia, *Trivia arctica* (Pulteney, 1799). Shell globular, solid, resembling the Nun Trivia, but smaller, with fewer ribs, pinkish, and lacking the dorsal spots. This species lives in deeper waters as well as intertidally. Its range extends from Norway to the Mediterranean.

Arctic Trivia
0.6 in (1.5 cm)

Flea Trivia, *Trivia pulex* (Link, 1807). Shell small, globular-elongate, pinkish brown, glossy on the top surface and whitish on the apertural side. Ribs very fine and numerous, with about eighteen to twenty on the columella. This is an intertidal warm-water species occurring in the Mediterranean, the Azores and north into Portugal.

Flea Trivia
0.3 in (1 cm)

Cowries and Bonnets
(*Families Cypraeidae and Cassidae*)

The cowrie family is limited to warm waters, but one species from the Mediterranean reaches north into Portugal. The colourful, glossy shell, with its narrow, toothed aperture, is made by the fleshy mantle that extends over the entire shell. There is no operculum.

The bonnets are small representatives of larger, tropical helmet shells of the family Cassidae.

Agate Cowrie, *Cypraea achatidea* Sowerby, 1837. Shell globular-elongate, glossy; upper surface with dense specklings and blotches of rich, dark-brown. Underside of shell and outer lip white. Teeth on either side of the narrow aperture are very small, the outer lip bearing about twenty to twenty-five. Uncommon in 3 to 100 ft (1–30 m). This is a southern species ranging from Portugal to West Africa.

Agate Cowrie
1.2 in (3 cm)

Rugose Bonnet, *Galeodea rugosa* (Linnaeus, 1771). Shell fairly thin but strong. Sculpture of fine spiral threads and with a single row of small round knobs on the shoulder. Aperture glossy-white, the inner wall quite wide, and the outer lip bearing a few, very small teeth. A common variable species of the Mediterranean but extends northward to the southern parts of the British Isles.

Rugose Bonnet
2.5 in (6 cm)

Mediterranean Bonnet, *Phalium granulatum* subspecies *undulatum* (Gmelin, 1791). Whorls bearing deep, thin, spiral grooves and with six or seven spiral rows of squarish, light-brown dots. Common in the Mediterranean and Azores, but rare as far north as Portugal.

Mediterranean Bonnet
3 in (7.5 cm)

✦

Moon Snails
(*Family Naticidae*)

The clam-eating moon snails are worldwide in distribution and are sand-dwellers, usually in shallow water. The operculum completely seals the aperture and may be soft and chitinous, as in *Neverita*, or may be hard and shelly, as in *Natica*. The females lay a circular, sand-covered collar into which the minute eggs are buried. In England they are called necklace-shells.

Drake's Moon Snail, *Neverita draconis* (Dall, 1903). Shell globular, with well-rounded, greyish whorls. Umbilicus quite wide and deep. The upper part of the columella has a very small, swollen callus. The periostracum is absent on the whorls, but often remaining within the umbilicus. A southern offshore species ranging from Baja California to Oregon.

Drake's Moon Snail
2.4 in (6 cm)

Shark Eye, *Neverita duplicata* (Say, 1822). A slightly flattened, globular, glossy, grey shell characterized by a deep umbilicus covered over by a large, button-like, brown callus. Columella white. A common, shallow-water sand-flat species with a large plough-like forefoot and reduced tentacles. Ranges from Massachusetts to Texas.

Shark Eye
2.5 in (6.5 cm)

Josephine's Moon Snail, *Neverita josephinia* (Risso, 1826). Globular, but flattened from above; glossy grey to yellowish brown above and whitish underneath. Aperture chocolate. Umbilicus filled by a brown, flattened callus. A Mediterranean sandflat-dweller, ranging north into Portugal.

Josephine's Moon Snail
1.5 in (4 cm)

Spotted Northern Moon Snail, *Lunatia triseriata* (Say, 1822). A small, drab, globular shell with a small, deep umbilicus. Usually covered by a dull, thin, tan periostracum. Colour of shell cream, the last whorl bears three spiral rows of twelve to fourteen bluish or reddish brown square spots. The borders of the sandy egg collar are crimped, rather than smooth as in *L. heros*. Common in shallow water to 100 ft (30 m) depth in coarse sand where it drills holes in small tellin clams. Ranges from eastern Canada to off North Carolina.

Spotted Northern Moon Snail
0.5 in (1.2 cm)

Common Northern Moon Snail, *Lunatia heros* (Say, 1822). Shell large, globular, relatively thin-shelled but strong. Umbilicus deep, round, not very large, and only slightly covered by a thickening of the columella wall. Colour dirty-white to brownish grey. Aperture glossy, tan or with purplish brown stains. Periostracum thin, light yellow-brown. Operculum chitinous, thin and light-brown. Egg case, with minute eggs embedded in it, is a wide, circular ribbon of sand, flexible when wet, but crumbles when dry. A common intertidal species ranging from the Gulf of St. Lawrence, Canada, to off North Carolina.

Common Northern Moon Snail
4 in (10 cm)

Lewis' Moon Snail, *Lunatia lewisi* (Gould, 1847). A heavy, globular shell, slightly shouldered a little distance below the suture. Umbilicus deep, round and narrow. Characterized by the brown-stained, rather small, button-like callus partially obscuring the top edge of the umbilicus. A very common clam-eating species found in 3 to 165 ft (1–50 m) of water from British Columbia to southern California.

Lewis' Moon Snail
4 in (10 cm)

European Necklace Shell, *Lunatia catena* (da Costa, 1776). Shell globular, with smooth, well-rounded whorls. Suture distinct. Umbilicus fairly large, deep and rounded. The upper half of the columella is swollen and glossy-white. Colour of shell tan with a row of slanting, short, dark-brown streaks just below the suture. Early whorls with a row of tan spots. Operculum chitinous and thin. Sandy egg collars wash ashore in the summer. A common, clam-eating dweller of intertidal sand-flats down to a depth of 410 ft (125 m). Ranges from the British Isles to the Mediterranean.

European Necklace Shell
1.5 in (4 cm)

Alder's Moon Snail, *Lunatia alderi* (Forbes, 1838). Shell small and globular with a short, depressed spire. Exterior glossy smooth. Umbilicus small, deep, partially covered by the brownish, glossy columella. Exterior tan with five spiral rows of chestnut-brown arrow-shaped, short streaks. The animal covers the shell with its foot. The forefoot, used for digging, covers the short tentacles and eyes. Lives from the intertidal sand-flats to deep, offshore waters where it feeds on tellin clams. Ranges from Norway south to the Mediterranean.

Alder's Moon Snail
0.6 in (1.5 cm)

Guillemin's Moon Snail, *Lunatia guillemini* (Payraudeau, 1826). Globular, with a pointed spire; exterior glossy smooth and solid. Umbilicus narrow and deep, bordered by a wide white band. Columella glossy, narrow, tinged with reddish brown. Aperture dark-brown. Colour bluish grey with numerous, dark-brown, intertwining streaks and lines. A common Mediterranean species extending north to the Brittany coast of France.

Guillemin's Moon Snail
1 in (2.5 cm)

Pale Northern Moon Snail, *Lunatia pallida* (Broderip and Sowerby, 1829). Globular, smooth, pure-white and covered with a thin, yellowish periostracum. Inner wall of aperture moderately thickened with a white glaze. Umbilicus almost closed. Operculum chitinous and translucent brown. A common, widely dispersed Arctic species found south to California and south to off North

Pale Northern Moon Snail
1.5 in (4 cm)

Carolina. Present in Scandinavia and rare in the North Sea. Lives on clay and sandy-mud bottoms from 32 to 6560 ft (10–2000 m).

Dusky Moon Snail, *Lunatia fusca* (Blainville, 1825). Shell small, globular with a low rounded spire. Colour brown to chestnut but, when fresh, covered with a dull, dark periostracum. Columella glossy, dark-brown with the base and lower aperture white. The columella is swollen where a spiral, rounded ridge emerges from the deep umbilicus. The soft parts are reddish brown. This is a southern Mediterranean species which extends northward into the British Isles wherever there is shallow water and a muddy sand bottom.

Dusky Moon Snail
1.2 in (3 cm)

Smith's Moon Snail, *Bulbus smithi* (Brown, 1839). Shell lightweight, globular, rather fragile, and with a bright straw-coloured or golden periostracum covering the shell, whose surface is minutely reticulated by spiral threads and growth lines. Aperture very large. Middle of columella is indented on the left. Uncommon offshore from Labrador to the Georges Banks of Massachusetts.

Smith's Moon Snail
1 in (2.5 cm)

Iceland Moon Snail, *Amauropsis islandicus* (Gmelin, 1791). Shell globular, somewhat lightweight, with a strongly channeled suture. The rounded, smooth whorls are covered with a thin, yellowish brown periostracum which flakes off when dry. Umbilicus absent or only a slight slit. Columella narrow and glossy white. Operculum with few whorls, chitinous and

Iceland Moon Snail
1.3 in (3 cm)

translucent brown and with microscopic spiral lines. A moderately common, cold-water moon snail found just offshore down to 525 ft (160 m). It is a circumpolar species extending south to off Virginia and to the North Sea and Scandinavia.

Purplish Moon Snail, *Amauropsis purpurea* Dall, 1871. Very similar to the Iceland Moon Snail but smaller and with a purplish-green periostracum and shallower sutural channels. Possibly only a subspecies which ranges from Alaska to British Columbia, Canada. Members of this genus lay a sandy egg collar in which are set single, large eggs which hatch into miniature, crawling snails. They feed on bivalves.

Purplish Moon Snail
0.7 in (2 cm)

Oldroyd's Fragile Moon Snail, *Calinaticina oldroydii* (Dall, 1897). Shell globular, rather thin-shelled, a little wider than high. Umbilicus wide and deep, with the upper part obscured by the expanded upper part of the white, glossy columella. Spiral lines on the outer shell are prominent. The species lives in large colonies in sandy areas offshore where they feed on small bivalves and lay sandy egg collars. Ranges from Oregon to southern California.

Oldroyd's Fragile Moon Snail
2.5 in (6 cm)

Arctic Natica, *Natica clausa* Broderip and Sowerby, 1829. Shell strong, fairly thin-shelled, smooth, yellowish white, with a smooth grey to yellowish brown periostracum. Whorls evenly well-rounded. Umbilicus sealed over by a small, glossy-white, flat callus. Operculum shelly, thin, slightly concave, smooth, white and with only a few whorls. Animal is translucent whitish cream with a large forefoot. A common circumpolar species extending southward through eastern Canada to off North Carolina; south to northern California; and from Scandinavia to off Portugal in deep water.

Arctic Natica
1 in (2.5 cm)

Dillwyn's Natica, *Naticarius dillwyni* (Payraudeau, 1826). Shell small, depressed globular, solid, glossy tan with white bands bearing obscure, arrowhead, chestnut-brown markings. Periostracum thin and yellowish brown. Umbilicus deep, narrow and partially covered by the glossy end of an umbilical cord. Operculum shelly, ivory-coloured, paucispiral and bordered by a deep groove and a raised spiral cord. Found on sand from 15 to 30 ft (4–10 m), from Portugal south into the Mediterranean.

Dillwyn's Natica
0.7 in (2 cm)

Fly-specked Natica, *Naticarius stercusmuscarum*, (Gmelin, 1791). Thin- but strong-shelled, smooth, globular, cream-coloured with numerous, irregularly placed, small dots of light-brown. Umbilicus fairly large and deep with a large, rounded spiral cord emerging from within and ending at the middle part of the narrow, glossy columella. Operculum shelly, dirty-white, with a dozen, distinct, sharp, crowded spiral ridges. Appears in Italian fish markets. A common shallow-water, Mediterranean species extending north into Portuguese waters.

Fly-specked Natica
2 in (5 cm)

Tritons and Dove-shells
(*Families Ranellidae and Columbellidae*)

Most members of the triton family, Ranellidae (formerly Cymatiidae), are warm-water dwellers, but one, the Oregon Triton, has ventured into the cold waters of northwest America. Cold-water forms have a thick, hairy periostracum. The numerous, small-shelled dove-shells are found worldwide, usually occurring as large colonies in shallow water. The operculum is chitinous and sickle-shaped. The foot narrow and the siphonal canal long. They are aggressive carnivores.

Oregon Triton, *Fusitriton oregonensis* (Redfield, 1848). Shell fusiform, with about six whorls, all convex in outline and bearing sixteen to eighteen axial riblets nodulated by the crossing of smaller spiral pairs of threads. The periostracum is heavy, spiculose, bristle-like and grey-brown. Common near shore from Alaska to British Columbia; in deeper water south to San Diego.

Oregon Triton
3 in (7.5 cm)

Variegated Dove-shell, *Astyris tuberosa* (Carpenter, 1865). Shell very small, slender, with a narrow, pointed, flat-sided spire; exterior smooth, usually glossy, tan with light-brown flames and spots. Outer lip thickened and with small teeth within. Common from 6 to 195 ft (2–60 m) from Alaska to California.

Variegated Dove-shell
0.4 in (8 mm)

Rosy Northern Dove-shell, *Astyris rosacea* (Gould, 1841). Very small, slender, dingy-white to rose, with a reddish apex. Smooth, except for microscopic spiral lines. A common circumboreal species found offshore in Alaska, Greenland to off New Jersey; and Norway to Portugal.

Rosy Northern Dove-shell
0.4 in (8 mm)

Lunar Dove-shell, *Astyris lunata* (Say, 1826). Shell very small, glossy, smooth, translucent grey and marked with fine, axial zigzag brown to yellow stripes. Base of shell with fine incised lines. Aperture constricted and slightly sinuate. Outer lip with four small teeth on the inside. No prominent varix. Nuclear whorls very small and translucent. A very common, shallow-water species associated with weedy areas. Ranges from southern Massachusetts to Texas and to Brazil.

Lunar Dove-shell
0.2 in (5 mm)

Joseph's Coat Amphissa, *Amphissa versicolor* Dall, 1871. Shell elongate to ovate, rather thin-shelled but strong; with seven glossy whorls which bear about fifteen obliquely slanting, strong, rounded axial ribs. Numerous spiral, incised lines are strongest on the base of the body whorl. Lower columella area has a small shield. Outer lip thickened within by about a dozen small, white teeth. Colour pinkish grey with indistinct mottlings of orange-brown. This is a common intertidal species found as deep as 65 ft (20 m). Occurs from British Columbia to off Baja California.

Joseph's Coat Amphissa
0.5 in (1.2 cm)

Columbian Amphissa, *Amphissa columbiana* Dall, 1916. Similar to Joseph's Coat Amphissa but twice as large and with twenty to twenty-four weaker, vertical, axial riblets on the last whorl. There is a low, rounded varix behind the outer lip. Colour yellow-brown with indistinct mauve mottlings. Periostracum thin and yellowish. Operculum chitinous and brown. Moderately common in shallow water from Alaska to Oregon; rarely off the southern Californian coast.

Columbian Amphissa
1 in (2.5 cm)

✦

Murex and Rock Shells
(*Family Muricidae*)

This is a very diverse and widely distributed family of carnivorous snails. The sexes are separate, and they have a strong set of radular teeth and a tough, horny operculum. Eggs are laid in clusters or balls of leathery capsules.

Purple Dye Murex, *Bolinus brandaris* (Linnaeus, 1758). Shell with a swollen body whorl, ovate aperture and a long, straight siphonal canal. Sculpture of two rows of about six or seven strong, short, straight spines on each whorl. The species is mainly Mediterranean, but is found as far north as Portugal.

Purple Dye Murex
2.5 in (6 cm)

Trunculus Murex, *Hexaplex trunculus* (Linnaeus, 1758). Shell broadly fusiform, with a short, broad siphonal canal twisted to the left. Axial ribs and former lips have an open spine at the shoulder. Colour brownish with two or three narrow, spiral bands of white. It is common in the Mediterranean, and rare as far north as Portugal.

Trunculus Murex
2 in (5 cm)

Foliated Thorn Purpura, *Ceratostoma foliatum* (Gmelin, 1791). Solid, heavy shell with three large, thin, foliaceous varices per whorl which are finely fimbriated on the anterior side. Numerous small spiral cords present. Siphonal canal closed along its length, its tip turned up. Base of outer lip with a small, strong spine. Exterior white to light-brown. Found on rocks near shore, where it feeds on mussels and barnacles, commonly from southern Alaska to northern California.

Foliated Thorn Drupa
2.5 in (6 cm)

Atlantic Oyster Drill, *Urosalpinx cinerea* (Say 1822). Broadly fusiform, without axial varices but having about nine to eleven rounded, axial ribs per whorl and with numerous, strong spiral cords. Outer lip slightly thickened on the inside and sometimes with two to six small, whitish teeth. Colour a dirty-grey or yellowish with irregular, brown spiral bands. Aperture brown. This common, shallow-water species is very destructive to oysters. Ranges from Nova Scotia to northeast Florida. Introduced prior to 1888 to Washington and central California. Later introduced to England.

Atlantic Oyster Drill
0.8 in (2 cm)

Lurid Dwarf Triton, *Urosalpinx lurida* (Middendorff, 1848). Fusiform, with rounded whorls, elongate spire, and numerous, rough, rounded spiral cords crossing eight to ten weak, rounded axial ribs. Six to eight small teeth are on the inside of the outer lip. Colour variable, whitish to rusty-brown, sometimes banded. Periostracum dark-brown and fuzzy. Siphonal canal usually sealed along its length. Very common in rocky intertidal areas from southern Alaska to northern California; rarer to the south.

Lurid Dwarf Triton
1 in (2.5 cm)

Spindle Dwarf Triton, *Urosalpinx fusulus* (Brocchi, 1814). Shell fusiform; six whorls, slightly shouldered, with nine or ten rounded, axial ribs crossed by numerous, spiral cords which form two rows of low tubercles in the whorls in the spire. Siphonal canal fairly long, open along its length. Columella glossy white. Inside of outer lip with four or five strong, short teeth. Suture well-indented. Spire pointed; nuclear whorls brown and glassy. Aperture darker within. Operculum chitinous, heavy and brown. Moderately common in rocky shallow areas in the Mediterranean and western Europe.

Spindle Dwarf Triton
0.8 in (2 cm)

Edwards' Dwarf Winkle, *Ocinebrina edwardsii* (Payraudeau, 1826). Shell small, broadly fusiform, six whorls, slightly shouldered. Sculpture of about sixteen elongate, rounded axial ribs per whorl crossed by numerous, fine, irregular threads, usually a lighter tan. Columella smooth, stained glossy tan. Inside swollen outer lip are six or seven short teeth. Siphonal canal short, closed off on apertural side. Interior of aperture purplish tan. A shallow-water, hard-bottom species common in the Mediterranean and northward into Portugal.

Edwards' Dwarf Winkle
0.8 in (2 cm)

Sharp Dwarf Winkle, *Ocinebrina aciculata* (Lamarck, 1822). Shell small, broadly fusiform, heavily ornamented with eight to ten slanting, rounded, axial ribs crossed by delicately fimbriated, spiral threads. Siphonal canal short, usually closed along its length. Six or seven elongated teeth are within the outer lip. Spire pointed. Colour tan to orange-buff. Umbilicus chink-like. Soft parts red with flecks of yellow. They probably feed upon small, intertidal barnacles. Common from southern British Isles to the Mediterranean.

Sharp Dwarf Winkle
0.7 in (2 cm)

Spotted Thorn Drupe, *Acanthina spirata* (Blainville, 1832). Low-spired, solid, smoothish, except for numerous, poorly-developed, spiral threads. Spine on lower outer lip is strong, behind which on the base of the outside of the body whorl is a weak spiral groove. Whorls slightly shouldered. Colour bluish grey with numerous rows of small, red-brown dots. Aperture within is bluish white. Rarely, all-yellow forms occurs. Common at high-tide mark along rocky shores and among beds of mussels upon which they feed. Ranges from Puget Sound, Washington, to southern California.

Spotted Thorn Drupe
1.2 in (3 cm)

Crested Dwarf Triton, *Muricopsis cristatus* (Brocchi, 1814). Shell slender and fusiform with a pointed spire and slightly shouldered whorls. Low axial rounded ribs are made knobby because of spiral cords. Colour brown with two broad spiral bands of yellowish. Columella pinkish, glossy and with two indistinct beads near the bottom. Outer lip thick and recurved, and with three coarse white teeth. Siphonal canal fairly long and open along its length. Intertidal rocky areas in the Mediterranean to Senegal and to southern Portugal.

Crested Dwarf Triton
1 in (2.5 cm)

Thick-lipped Drill, *Eupleura caudata* (Say, 1822). Shell fusiform and dorso-ventrally compressed and with two lateral varices. Apex pointed; siphonal canal moderately long, almost closed, coming to a sharp point below. Last varix large, rounded and with small nodules. Inside of outer lip with about six small, bead-like teeth. Whorls with small spiral cords and strong axial ribs. There are four to six axial ribs between the last two varices. An abundant shallow-water species that feeds by boring into young oysters. Ranges from south of Cape Cod to northern Florida.

Thick-lipped Drill
1 in (2.5 cm)

Frilled Dogwinkle, *Nucella lamellosa* (Gmelin, 1791). Solid, with a fairly high spire. Columella almost vertical and straight, not flattened. Sculpturing and colour very variable: white, greyish, cream or orange, sometimes spirally banded. Smoothish or with foliated ribs. Sometimes spinose. A very common rock-loving species

Frilled Dogwinkle
2 in (5 cm)

extending from the Bering Straits, Alaska, to central California.

Atlantic Dogwinkle, *Nucella lapillus* (Linnaeus, 1758). Broadly fusiform; spire usually elevated. Exterior either smoothish or sculptured with rounded, spiral ridges which may be finely fimbriated. Colour usually dull-white, but in many specimens yellowish, orange or brownish. Rarely with dark-brown spiral bands. In some areas of New England there are colonies of strongly fimbriated specimens. This abundant species lives on rocky coasts between tide marks where it feeds upon barnacles and small mussels. The animal gives off a tyrian purple dye once used as an indelible laundry marking ink. The species ranges from southern Labrador to New York; from Norway to northern Portugal.

Atlantic Dogwinkle
1.5 in (4 cm)

Emarginate Dogwinkle, *Nucella emarginata* (Deshayes, 1839). With a rather short spire. Aperture large. Columella strongly arched, flattened and slightly concave below. Sculpturing variable, but characteristically with coarse spiral cords, usually alternatingly small and large. Cords often scaled or coarsely noduled. Exterior dirty-grey to rusty-brown, sometimes with darker spiral bands. Aperture and columella light-brown. A very common rock-dwelling, coastal species ranging from Alaska to southern California.

Emarginate Dogwinkle
1 in (2.5 cm)

File Dogwinkle, *Nucella lima* (Gmelin, 1791). Broadly fusiform, with a low spire, rounded whorls with seventeen to twenty round-topped, smooth, crowded spiral cords, the latter often alternating in size. Colour whitish or orange-brown, rarely banded. This is a common, cold-water, intertidal species ranging from northern Japan and Alaska to northern California.

File Dogwinkle
1.2 in (3 cm)

Channeled Dogwinkle, *Nucella canaliculata* (Duclos, 1832). Shell solid, elongate-globose, with about fourteen to sixteen low, flat-topped, closely spaced spiral cords on the body whorl. Suture slightly channeled. Colour white or orange-brown, often spirally banded. This is a moderately common intertidal species feeding on mussels and barnacles in rocky areas. Ranges from the Aleutian Islands to central California.

Channeled Dogwinkle
1 in (2.5 cm)

Sting Winkle, *Ocenebra erinacea* (Linnaeus, 1758). Shell broadly fusiform with an angulate, acute spire. Whorls shouldered and sculptured by seven or eight thin, erect, evenly spaced axial ribs, crossed by numerous, rounded, finely fimbriated cords. Siphonal canal closed along its length and fairly long, with a scarred siphonal fasciole alongside. Aperture oval. Outer lip often bounded by a thin, well-developed varix. Exterior yellowish, often with brown bandings. Common below low tide mark in rocky areas where they feed on bivalves. In the spring they lay clusters of urn-shaped egg capsules. Ranges from southern British Isles to the Azores and the Mediterranean.

Sting Winkle
1.5 in (4 cm)

Poulson's Dwarf Triton, *Ocenebra poulsoni* (Carpenter, 1864). Shell solid, with a semi-gloss finish. Whorls with eight or nine nodulated, rounded, axial ribs per whorl crossed by numerous, very fine, incised spiral lines on the ribs. Siphonal canal narrowly open. Periostracum thin, greyish or brownish and smooth. Aperture white. A very common species on rocks and wharf pilings, especially in the southern part of its range, from California to Mexico.

Poulson's Dwarf Triton
1.5 in (4 cm)

Clathrate Trophon, *Boreotrophon clathratus* (Linnaeus, 1758). Shell fusiform, dull-white, with a deep suture which may have a flat area just below it. Siphonal canal well-developed and open along its side. Whorls with strong, thin axial ribs which are hollow in front. In many specimens the tops of the ribs are rounded, but in others they may be protruding up into small projections. Aperture white, and outer lip slightly flaring. Young specimens have a fairly long siphonal canal. A moderately common dweller of mud bottoms offshore in Arctic Seas. It extends into the waters of Maine and Norway.

Clathrate Trophon
1.5 in (4 cm)

Northwest Pacific Trophon, *Boreotrophon pacificus* (Dall, 1902). Shell white, fusiform, similar to the Clathrate Trophon, but the length of the aperture and siphonal canal is more than half the length of the entire shell. The well-rounded whorls have twelve to twenty ribs which are slightly shouldered just below the well-indented suture. This carnivorous species is fairly

Northwest Pacific Trophon
1 in (2.5 cm)

common at the low tide area in Alaska, but further south it is found offshore in deep water. It also occurs in Canadian Arctic waters.

Stuart's Trophon, *Boreotrophon stuarti* (E. A. Smith, 1880). Broadly fusiform, pure-white to yellow-cream and with a waxy texture. Each of the five or six whorls has nine to eleven strong, thin, lamella-like, high-shouldered ribs. Whorls in the spire are cancellated by two or three spiral raised threads. Body whorl with five very weak spiral, rounded threads. Uncommon from low tide down to about 165 ft (50 m). Extends from Alaska to off San Diego, California.

Stuart's Trophon
2 in (5 cm)

Alaskan Trophon, *Boreotrophon alaskanus* (Dall, 1902). Shell cream-white, fusiform, with the whorls almost detached. The suture is very deep and there is a flat, spiral gutter adjacent to it. There are about nine varices per whorl with the tops extending upwards in the form of open flutes. Siphonal canal fairly long. This attractive species ranges from northern Japan to the Bering Sea in deep water.

Alaskan Trophon
1.3 in (3 cm)

Truncate Trophon, *Boreotrophon truncatus* (Strom, 1768). Shell white, fusiform with a sharp conical spire. Suture deep and bounded below by a slightly flattened, narrow gutter. Fifteen to twenty-five ribs on the last whorl, strongest at the top and fading out towards the base of the shell. Colour yellowish brown.

Columella and aperture glossy-white. Outer lip thin and smooth. No umbilicus. A common, cold-water, circumpolar species occurring in offshore waters south to the Georges Banks, Massachusetts; Alaska; Greenland south to the Bay of Biscay, France.

Truncate Trophon
0.6 in (1.5 cm)

Latticed Trophon, *Boreotrophon craticulatus* (Fabricius, 1780). Shell fusiform, of a creamy waxy consistency with the top of the whorls shouldered and bearing about ten delicate, thin, semi-translucent, axial varices. There are numerous very small spiral cords that cross the riblets and give the shell a slightly latticed appearance. Aperture half the length of the entire shell and narrowing below into a fairly short, open siphonal canal. Nuclear whorls distinct, bulbous and glassy smooth. *B. fabricii* (Moller, 1842) is a synonym. It lives in about 196 ft (60 m) of water from Arctic Canada to Nova Scotia.

Latticed Trophon
1 in (2.5 cm)

✦

Buccinum Whelks
(Family Buccinidae)

This is a family of large, cold-water univalves, known in England as buckies and whelks. They are offshore-dwellers, many of which are found in fish markets and also serve as food for bottom-feeding fish. All have a chitinous, brown operculum.

Common Northern Buccinum or **Buckie**, *Buccinum undatum* Linnaeus, 1758, is the best known of the northern edible whelks. Shell solid, chalky-grey to yellowish brown, with a moderately thick, grey periostracum. Axial ribs slanting, nine to eighteen per whorl, low, rounded and extending quarter to half the way down the whorl. Common in shallow water in the lower Arctic Seas as far south as New Jersey and the British Isles.

Common Northern Buccinum
3 in (7.5 cm)

Totten's Buccinum, *Buccinum totteni* Stimpson, 1865. Thin-shelled, with five or six large, well-rounded, smoothish whorls. Aperture slightly less than half the length of the shell. Colour yellow-brown with a thin, straw-coloured periostracum. Spiral sculpture of numerous, finely incised striations. Ranges from Arctic Canada to Maine; Greenland and Iceland.

Totten's Buccinum
2 in (5 cm)

Plectrum Buccinum, *Buccinum plectrum* Stimpson, 1865. Shell thin-shelled but strong. Aperture about one third the length of the shell. Numerous axial, rounded ribs slanting and limited to the upper third of the whorl. Spiral sculpture of numerous, crowded, rough threads. Colour greyish to yellowish white. Common offshore in Arctic waters south to Puget Sound; and south to the Gulf of St. Lawrence, Canada.

Plectrum Buccinum
2.5 in (6 cm)

Glacial Buccinum, *Buccinum glaciale* Linnaeus, 1761. A fairly thick, sturdy shell, but lightweight in comparison to its size. Characterized by its thick, glossy, white, flaring, reflected outer lip, and by the two wavy, strong spiral cords on the periphery of the whorls. Spiral incised lines numerous. Suture narrow and deep. Colour mauve-brown. Aperture cream with a purplish flush within. Common from low tide to several feet. Ranges in the Arctic Seas to Washington State and south to the Gulf of St. Lawrence.

Glacial Buccinum
2.5 in (6 cm)

Angulate Buccinum, *Buccinum angulosum* Gray, 1839. Shell solid, similar to the Glacial Buccinum, but with a shorter spire. Aperture half the length of the entire shell. Early whorls smooth. Post-nuclear whorls with numerous, rounded axial ribs extending from suture to suture. Later whorls with fewer, widely spaced, short, slanting ribs which are sometimes stained rusty-brown. Between the ribs the shell is slightly concave and may bear one or two weak spiral threads. Columella enamel-white, slightly twisted below. Outer lip flaring, thickened and smooth. Occurs in the European and Canadian Arctic waters as well as the Bering Straits.

Angulate Buccinum
2.5 in (6 cm)

Finmark Buccinum, *Buccinum finmarkianum* Verkrüzen, 1875. Shell oblong-ovate, thin-shelled, smooth, yellowish white with a thin, yellowish periostracum. Whorls well-rounded. Sculpture sometimes with very faint spiral threads. Suture neatly indented. Columella and aperture enamel-white. Outer lip thin, smooth and slightly flaring below. Operculum small, almost circular, chitinous and translucent yellow. An

Finmark Buccinum
2.5 in (6 cm)

uncommon species found off Norway.

Silky Buccinum, *Buccinum scalariforme* Moller, 1842. Aperture half the length of the entire shell. Whorls in spire and the upper two-thirds of the last whorl with numerous, strong, narrow, slanting, axial ribs which are sometimes intertwining. Outer lip slightly sinuate, thin and slightly flaring. Spiral sculpture of microscopic, beaded threads giving the surface a silky appearance. Colour light-brown but covered with a dark, thin periostracum. *B. tenue* Gray is a synonym. Common offshore down to 655 ft (200 m). Arctic Seas to Washington State; and south to the Gulf of Maine.

Silky Buccinum
2 in (5 cm)

Polar Buccinum, *Buccinum polare* Gray, 1839. Similar to the Silky Buccinum, but the shell is more globose, with a lower spire and broader, more flaring, sharper, smooth outer lip. Axial riblets more numerous, much smaller, and crossed by numerous spiral threads which form distinct beads and a latticed effect. Columella and aperture glossy yellowish white. Periostracum thin, light-brown. A cold-water circumpolar species extending southward to northern Japan, Alaska and to Greenland.

Polar Buccinum
2.5 in (6 cm)

Flaky Buccinum, *Buccinum hydrophanum* Hancock, 1846. Shell with a tall spire, an aperture about one third the length of the entire shell. Whorls rounded, smoothish. Siphonal fasciole absent. Fine growth lines may be present. Outer lip thin, sharp and flaring somewhat below. Colour pale yellowish brown. This carnivorous species lives from 330 to 3935 ft (100–1200 m) on muddy bottoms. It is an Arctic species ranging across Canada to the Grand Banks and in Europe south to the Shetland Islands.

Flaky Buccinum
3 in (7.5 cm)

Humphrey's Buccinum, *Buccinum humphreysianum* Bennett, 1824. Thin-shelled, broadly oval with smoothish, well-rounded whorls. Spire regularly conic, the aperture about half the length of the entire shell. Siphonal canal short and wide. Outer lip thin and fragile. Surface with extremely fine spiral threads crossed by fine, slanting growth lines. Periostracum very thin, yellowish with occasional weak brownish streaks. An uncommon, deep-water species found in Arctic Seas in Japan, Canada and northwestern Europe as far south as off Portugal.

Humphrey's Buccinum
3 in (7.5 cm)

Baer's Buccinum, *Buccinum baeri* (Middendorff, 1848). Shell small, ovate-elongate, smoothish, with a beachworn appearance. Aperture a little more than half the length of the shell. Spiral sculpture of very weak, smooth, narrow threads. Growth lines crude on the last whorl. Exterior colour light-brown. Range is from the Aleutians to Kodiak Island, Alaska.

Baer's Buccinum
1.5 in (4 cm)

Finely-striate Buccinum, *Buccinum striatissimum* Sowerby, 1899. Shell fairly large, relatively thin-shelled, whitish, with a high acute spire and an aperture one third the length of the shell. Whorls very well-rounded, the suture well-indented. Surface covered with very fine spiral threads. Growth lines weak, but made more evident when the thin, grey periostracum is worn away. Siphonal notch short, narrow but distinct. Interior of aperture white. Occurs in deep water from Japan to Alaska; uncommon.

Finely-striate Buccinum
3.5 in (9 cm)

Norwegian Volute Whelk, *Volutopsius norvegicus* (Gmelin, 1791). Shell large, copious, with a tall spire and a large aperture about half the length of the shell. Whorls well-rounded, smoothish, except for very fine growth lines. Suture finely indented and sometimes with small wrinkles below it. Outer lip smooth, enamel-white and reflected in the upper half. The lower edge is confluent with the hardly evident siphonal region. It is moderately common in cold water south to the Gulf of St. Lawrence; Newfoundland; Scotland and Scandinavia.

Norwegian Volute Whelk
5 in (12.5 cm)

Melon Volute Whelk, *Volutopsius melonis* (Dall, 1891). Shell large, spire short, aperture two-thirds the length of the shell. Two nuclear whorls, smooth, white. Remainder of whorls have crowded, well-rounded, straight, axial ribs crossed by very numerous, crowded, rounded, rough spiral threads. Colour ashen purplish grey with a white, narrow columella. An uncommon deep-water species from northern Japan and the Bering Sea.

Melon Volute Whelk
5 in (12.5 cm)

Chestnut Buccinum, *Volutopsius castaneus* (Mörch, 1858). Shell fusiform, rather solid, with four whorls, the early one being bulbous and smooth. Aperture large, slightly larger than half the length of the shell and slightly flaring above. Siphonal canal weakly defined. Exterior surface brownish and smoothish, except for coarse axial wrinkles appearing more as deformities. Moderately common on rocks offshore from the Aleutians to Kodiak Islands, Alaska.

Chestnut Volute Whelk
3 in (7.5 cm)

Sinistral Arctic Whelk, *Pyrolofusus deformis* (Reeve, 1847) is one of the few normally "left-handed" or sinistrally coiling whelks in the northern hemisphere. Shell solid, sinistral, whitish grey, with many low, irregular spiral cords. Nuclear whorls bulbous. Aperture with a thin slightly waved outer lip and enamel-white with brown staining within. Uncommon offshore in the Arctic Seas; Alaska, Greenland and northwestern Europe.

Sinistral Arctic Whelk
3 in (7.5 cm)

Behring's Neptune, *Beringion behringi* (Middendorff, 1844). Shell large, fusiform, dextral, with four or five well-rounded whorls, the first two smooth and bulbous, but usually badly eroded. Suture coarsely indented. Aperture slightly more than half the length of entire shell. Siphonal canal well-developed but short. Outer lip not flaring, but thin, smooth and strong. Exterior has five or six weak spiral cords and weak, coarse, low ribs. There is an eroded look to this purplish brown

Behring's Neptune
3 in (7.5 cm)

shell. Formerly called *Beringius beringi*. Uncommon offshore in the Bering Sea.

Kennicott's Neptune, *Beringion kennicottii* (Dall, 1907). Shell large, not very heavy. Characterized by about nine strong, arched, somewhat rounded axial ribs extending from suture to suture and, on the body whorl, extending three-quarters the way down. Spiral sculpture of microscopic scratches, except on the base where there are a dozen or so weak threads. Periostracum light-brown, thin and usually flakes off from dried specimens. Shell chalky-grey. Moderately common offshore from 9 to 165 ft (3–50 m) from the Aleutians to Cook's Inlet, Alaska.

Kennicott's Neptune
3.5 in (9 cm)

Turton's Neptune, *Neoberingius turtoni* (Bean, 1834). Shell large, broadly fusiform, thin-shelled but strong; two nuclear whorls bulbous, white and smooth. Spire acute, tall, with well-rounded whorls bearing numerous, weakly beaded spiral threads. Aperture less than half the length of the entire shell. Outer lip thin, sharp but strong. Siphonal canal produced below and open. Colour whitish grey. *B. ossiani* (Friele, 1879) is a synonym. Moderately common offshore in the Arctic Seas, Scandinavia south to the North Sea; Labrador to Newfoundland and the Gulf of St. Lawrence.

Turton's Neptune
5 in (12.5 cm)

Pygmy Colus, *Colus pygmaeus* (Gould, 1841). Shell small, fusiform, fairly fragile, with a straight-sided, pointed apex and with rounded whorls. Exterior chalk-white, with numerous fine spiral threads covered with a light olive-grey, thin, smoothish periostracum. Aperture about half the length of the shell. This is one of several boreal species of *Colus* found in the northern hemisphere. This small one extends offshore from the Gulf of St. Lawrence to off North Carolina.

Pygmy Colus
0.8 in (2 cm)

Hairy Colus, *Colus pubescens* (Verrill, 1882). Shell of moderate size, fusiform, solid, with a straight-sided spire. It is similar to the Pygmy Colus, but larger, with a longer aperture and the sutures are not as deeply impressed nor as wide. Spiral sculpture of numerous, crowded incised lines. Periostracum dark-brown, thin, velvety when wet but flakes off when dry. Very commonly dredged from 100 to 3940 ft (30–1200 m) from Arctic Canada to off South Carolina.

Hairy Colus
2.5 in (6 cm)

Simple Colus, *Colus gracilis* (da Costa, 1778). Shell fusiform, elongate, with a tall, straight-sided spire. Protoconch smooth, slightly swollen. Whorls moderately convex and with about sixty low, spiral threads, crossed occasionally by axial growth lines. Aperture oval, cream-white. Columella enamel-white, arched. Siphonal canal fairly long and twisted slightly to the left. Colour of shell white, with a yellowish brown, soft periostracum. *C. glaber* (Kobelt) is a synonym. Lives on sandy mud bottoms from 100 to 1970 ft (30-600 m) deep from Norway to off Portugal.

Simple Colus
2.7 in (7 cm)

Spitzbergen Colus, *Colus spitzbergeni* (Reeve, 1855). Spindle-shaped, rather light-shelled. Spire elongate. Whorls well-rounded with twelve to fourteen small, low, flat-topped, equally sized, spiral cords. Periostracum thin, reddish brown. Common offshore from 6 to 852 ft (2–260 m). Arctic Seas to Maine and Scandinavia; Bering Sea to Washington State.

Spitzbergen Colus
3 in (7.5 cm)

Jeffrey's Colus, *Colus jeffreysianus* (Fischer, 1868). Shell fusiform, similar to the Simple Colus, but fatter and with a proportionately longer aperture. The siphonal canal is shorter. Spiral sculpture coarser, with about thirty spiral threads on the last whorl. Shell white, rarely with a pinkish brown tint. Periostracum pale-yellow. A synonym appears to be *turgidulus* (Friele). This carnivorous snail lives on sandy mud bottoms from 195 to 2295 ft (60–700 m). Ranges from Norway to off Spain.

Jeffrey's Colus
2 in (5 cm)

Iceland Colus, *Colus islandicus* (Gmelin, 1791). Shell broadly fusiform. Three nuclear whorls, bulbous, and set obliquely to the rest of the shell. Whorls slightly convex. Siphonal canal long and almost straight. Outer lip thin and strong. Surface whitish, with numerous, fine, subdued, spiral ridges and covered by a pale brownish, smooth periostracum. Aperture about half the length of the shell. Outer lip thin, smooth and strong. These carnivorous snails live on sandy mud bottoms from 32 to 9840 ft (10–3000 m) deep. They lay a leathery, dome-

Iceland Colus
5 in (12.5 cm)

shaped capsule on rocks and each may contain several thousand minute eggs. Ranges in the Arctic Seas from Canada to Scandinavia.

Stimpson's Colus, *Colus stimpsoni* (Mörch, 1867). Fusiform, very similar to the Iceland Colus, but is fatter and has a less produced nuclear whorl. Shell chalky-white, but covered with a semi-glossy, light- to dark-brown, moderately thin periostracum. Sculpture of numerous incised spiral lines. Fairly common from 9 to 3280 ft (3–1000 m). Found off Labrador and Newfoundland south to off North Carolina.

Stimpson's Colus
4 in (10 cm)

Herendeen's Colus, *Colus herendeenii* (Dall, 1902). Shell elongate-fusiform with about seven whorls that are slightly convex. Aperture ovate and less than half the length of the entire shell. Sutures narrow and very deep. Whorls with numerous, deep incised lines, between which are formed flat-topped, narrow spiral cords. Siphonal canal moderately long. Colour white and overlaid by a thin, yellowish periostracum. Uncommon off the Aleutian Islands and eastward to the Shumagin Islands, Alaska, in fairly deep water.

Herendeen's Colus
2.7 in (7 cm)

Fat Colus, *Colus ventricosus* (Gmelin, 1791). Shell fusiform but very fat, with well-rounded whorls and an aperture that is slightly longer than half the entire shell. Spiral sculpture of very faint, raised lines. Siphonal canal open along its length and slightly twisted. Outer lip thin, sharp and strong. Colour of shell whitish grey. Periostracum velvety, brownish and fairly thick. Uncommon offshore from Nova Scotia to the Georges Banks, Massachusetts.

Fat Colus
2 in (5 cm)

Ovum Arctic Whelk, *Liomesus ovum* (Turton, 1825). Shell fairly small, ovate-fusiform, smooth, creamy white, and with convex whorls. Nuclear whorls very small. Growth lines not apparent unless the outer lip had been previously broken. Columella short, and with an abrupt twist at the end. Outer lip slightly flaring and round at the base. Parietal wall with a large, glazed white area. Periostracum very thin and translucent. Small round leathery capsules are fastened in a clump to the underside of the female's shell. One of many eggs develops into a single large, crawling young snail. Synonym: *L. dalei* (Sowerby, 1825). It is common in the northern waters of northwestern Europe.

Ovum Arctic Whelk
1.5 in (4 cm)

Common Northwest Neptune, *Neptunea lyrata* (Gmelin, 1791). Shell large, broadly fusiform, solid, fairly heavy. With five or six strongly convex whorls bearing about eight strongly to poorly developed, raised spiral cords, two of which usually are seen in each whorl in the spire. Faint spiral threads are also present. Exterior dull whitish brown. Fairly common in Alaska from shore to 330 ft (100 m); off Oregon and northern California it occurs in deeper water.

Common Northwest Neptune
5 in (12.5 cm)

Disreputable Neptune, *Neptunea despecta* (Linnaeus, 1758). Fusiform, usually appearing worn and unattractive. Colour dingy-white or brownish tan. Eight whorls very convex, the last being ventricose. Sometimes spirally banded with light-chestnut. Spiral sculpture of fine, crowded threads. Upper whorls usually have two large, crude spiral cords which gradually disappear on the body whorl. Aperture just less than half the length of the shell and somewhat flaring. This species is quite variable and has had many subspecies described. It is found offshore in deep water from Arctic Canada to Maine and in Scandinavia and the Shetland Islands.

Disreputable Neptune
3 in (7.5 cm)

New England Neptune, *Neptunea lyrata* subspecies *decemcostata* (Say, 1826). Broadly fusiform, solid. Characterized by its greyish white, rather smooth shell which bears seven to ten very strong, squarish, reddish brown, spiral cords. The upper whorls show two or three cords. There is an additional band of brown just below the suture. This is a common soft-bottom carnivore found offshore and distributed from off Nova Scotia to off North Carolina.

A form or possibly subspecies, *N. lyrata turnerae* A. H. Clarke, 1956, has a shorter spire and broader shell. It ranges from Grand Manan Island, New Brunswick, to Mount Desert Island, Maine.

New England Neptune
4 in (10 cm)

Clench's Neptune, *Neptunea despecta* subspecies *clenchi* A. H. Clarke, 1956. Similar to the Disreputable Neptune, but more elongate, with a higher spire and much stronger spiral cords. The siphonal canal is not as twisted although it is longer. It occurs along the northern Arctic areas of Canada.

Clench's Neptune
4 in (10 cm)

Phoenician Neptune, *Neptune lyrata* subspecies *phoenicea* (Dall, 1891). Elongate-fusiform, with five or six well-rounded whorls bearing numerous, small, raised, smooth, rounded spiral cords, seven on the upper whorls, twenty weaker ones on the body whorl. Colour of shell a uniform taffy-brown with lighter cords and threads. Aperture ovate, a little greater than half the length of the shell, slightly flaring, and blending in below with the short broad siphonal canal. Columella and inside of aperture white. Commonly dredged off the northern coast of British Columbia.

Phoenician Neptune
4 in (10 cm)

Ventricose Neptune, *Neptunea ventricosa* (Gmelin, 1791). Shell fat, heavy and solid. The swollen last whorl may bear weak or strong, rounded slanting axial ribs. Columella strongly twisted to the right. The siphonal fasciole often with scale-like fimbriations. Colour of shell a dirty-brownish white. Aperture white or flushed with brownish purple. Moderately common offshore. Ranges across the Arctic Ocean, especially in northern Alaska; also Scandinavia, northern Scotland and Iceland.

Ventricose Neptune
3.5 in (9 cm)

Ancient Neptune, *Neptunea antiqua* (Linnaeus, 1758). Large, strong shell, yellowish to grey, with weak, fine, spiral threads. Whorls rounded, swollen. Outer lip strong and smooth. Siphonal canal short, slightly twisted. A rare all-white form occurs in the North Sea. Sometimes specimens have a deep-orange mouth. Freaks may be sinistral. An edible species, common around the British Isles; Scandinavia and France; offshore to 6000 ft (1830 m).

Ancient Neptune
4 in (10 cm)

Contrary Neptune, *Neptunea contraria* (Linnaeus, 1771). Shell fusiform, sinistrally coiled, with a pointed spire, well-rounded whorls and a well-indented suture. Sculpture of numerous, crowded, squarish, raised, weakly beaded cords. Colour of shell a rich light-brown with a white aperture and siphonal canal. Outer lip slightly flaring and slightly crenulated. Operculum half size of the aperture, brown, chitinous, with a terminal nucleus. Moderately common offshore species from Portugal south into the Mediterranean.

Contrary Neptune
3.5 in (9 cm)

Smirnia Neptune, *Neptunea smirnia* (Dall, 1919). Fusiform, fairly large, with a large, slightly flaring aperture which is greater than half the entire length of the shell. Surface smoothish, except for four or five very weak, low, flat spiral cords on the early whorls. Last two whorls smooth-shouldered and with fine, faint, silky growth lines. Colour tan with a brown-stained aperture. A common soft-bottom species in

Smirnia Neptune
3.5 in (9 cm)

330 to 985 ft (100–300 m) of water. Occurs from northern Japan to Alaska and south off Washington State.

Heros Neptune, *Neptunea heros* (Gray, 1850). Shell large, heavy, fusiform with the shoulders angled by an irregular spiral cord. Axial ribs subdued and irregular. One spiral cord is usually prominent on the middle of the upper whorls. Scales on siphonal fasciole. Colour tawny-brown. Aperture whitish. Operculum chitinous, brown, almost as large as the aperture and its nucleus at the terminal end. Lives offshore in Arctic Seas from Japan to Alaska; uncommon.

Heros Neptune
4 in (10 cm)

Stiles Neptune, *Neptunea stilesi* A. G. Smith, 1968. Shell very broadly fusiform with a short spire and large last whorl. Outer lip not flaring. Siphonal canal relatively short. Columellar edge raised and glossy-white. Colour of shell dingy-white to tan or yellowish and occasionally reddish brown. Major sculpturing of widely spaced, distinct, rounded, low spiral cords which are darker brown. Uncommon from 223 to 820 ft (68–250 m). Ranges from off Vancouver Island, British Columbia, to Washington.

Stiles Neptune
4 in (10 cm)

Tabled Neptune, *Neptunea tabulata* (Baird, 1863). Shell fusiform, solid, with eight white whorls covered with a thin, brown periostracum. Characterized by the wide, flat channel next to the suture. It is bounded by a raised, scaly or fimbriated spiral cord. Remainder of whorl with

Tabled Neptune
3 in (7.5 cm)

numerous sandpapery spiral threads. Aperture white and one third the length of the entire shell. Siphonal canal moderately long, and sometimes with a very small, narrow, chink-like umbilicus. Moderately common offshore from 195 to 1310 ft (60–400 m), extending from British Columbia to San Diego, California.

Kroyer's Colus, *Plicifusus kroyeri* (Moller, 1842). Shell fusiform, with about seven rounded whorls bearing numerous, distinct, rounded, axial ribs. Suture narrowly and deeply indented. Exterior covered with a shiny, olive-brown periostracum. Aperture round, slightly less than half the length of the shell. Outer lip thin, slightly flaring. Columella has a built-up, narrow callus, and is quite twisted at the lower end. An offshore circumpolar species from the Bering Sea and Greenland to Norway.

Kroyer's Colus
3 in (7.5 cm)

Fenestrate Colus, *Siphonorbis fenestratus* (Turton, 1834). Somewhat fusiform, with a high spire of about seven slightly convex whorls. White, ovate aperture about one third the length of the shell. Siphonal canal short, slightly twisted. Suture strongly indented. Sculpture in upper whorls of numerous, rounded axial plicae crossed by several, smaller spiral threads. Nuclear whorls large and smooth. Colour of shell white. Animal creamy-white, siphon with many dark streaks. Alias *Turrisipho fusiformis* (Broderip, 1830), not Borson, 1820. Uncommon on gravel and sand bottoms. Ranges

Fenestrate Colus
1.6 in (4.5 cm)

from Newfoundland and Greenland to Scandinavia and rarely in the northern British Isles.

Ivory Colus, *Siphonorbis ebur* (Mörch, 1869). Similar to the Fenestrate Colus, but the spire is shorter, whorls more rounded, aperture about half the length of the shell, and lacking the axial ribs. Sculpture of numerous, irregularly placed, fine spiral threads crossed by even finer lines of growth. Siphonal canal short and slightly leaning to the left. Shell alabaster-white. Inhabits Arctic waters of northwest Scandinavia and Iceland.

Ivory Colus
3 in (7.5 cm)

Howse's Colus, *Siphonorbis howsei* (Marshall, 1911). Shell fusiform, solid, white, smoothish, except for weak, irregular spiral threads. Aperture about half the length of the entire shell. Suture finely indented. Outer lip thin, strong and smooth. Columella arched, the siphonal canal usually twisted to the left. Periostracum thin, translucent yellowish. Occurs offshore from 115 to 558 ft (35–170 m) in northwest Europe.

Howse's Colus
1.5 in (4 cm)

Destiny Colus, *Turrisipho lachesis* (Mörch, 1869). Shell elongate-fusiform, with about eight very rounded whorls. Spire high; aperture small, about quarter the length of the entire shell. Siphonal canal relatively short and narrow. Suture well-impressed. Axial sculpture absent. Whorls covered by numerous, crowded, small, flattish spiral cords. Colour of shell dirty-white; small aperture white

Destiny Colus
1.8 in (4.5 cm)

with a large brown, chitinous operculum. Periostracum, when present, is soft and grey. This uncommon carnivore lives on soft mud bottoms offshore in the area of Norway.

Ample Fragile Buccinum, *Volutharpa ampullacea* (Middendorff, 1848). Shell small, fragile, ovate and with a low spire. Aperture more than half the length of the shell; outer lip thin and flaring below. Siphonal canal short, its notch U-shaped. Nuclear whorl small and white. Four remaining whorls convex, smoothish. Colour of shell cream with broad axial streaks of yellow-brown or purplish. Suture slightly channeled. Periostracum thin, fuzzy, and greyish green. This is a moderately common, cold-water species living on gravel bottoms. It ranges from the Bering Sea to off British Columbia.

Ample Fragile Buccinum
1.5 in (4 cm)

Kellet's Whelk, *Kelletia kelleti* (Forbes, 1850). Shell very heavy and solid, broadly fusiform with a fine, wavy suture and a sharp, crimped outer lip. Whorls slightly concave between the suture and the shouldered periphery. The latter bears ten strong, rounded, elevated knobs per whorl. Base with about six to ten incised, spiral lines. Aperture glossy and white. Very common from northern California to Mexico in subtidal, rocky areas, as well as in Japan.

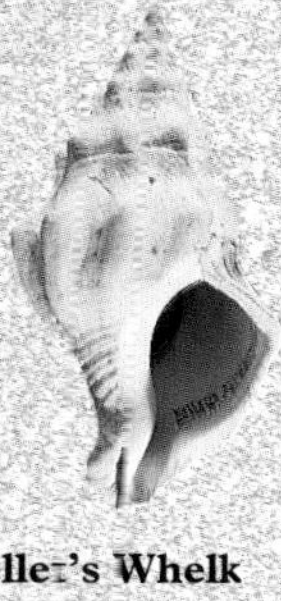

Kellet's Whelk
4 in (10 cm)

Dire Whelk, *Searlesia dira* (Reeve, 1846). Shell small, solid, fusiform with an acute spire, bearing nine to eleven low, rounded axial ribs.

Spiral sculpture of numerous, unequal-sized spiral threads. Aperture slightly more than half the length of the shell and coloured tan. Outer lip not flaring and made crenulate by the numerous, short, whitish spiral teeth just inside the aperture. Columella concave, thickened by an orange-brown, glossy callus. This is a common shallow-water species ranging from Alaska to Monterey, California.

Dire Whelk
1 in (2.5 cm)

Channeled Whelk, *Busycotypus canaliculatus* (Linnaeus, 1758). Shell fairly large, lightweight, fusiform with a relatively low spire and a large aperture that is three-quarters the length of the shell. Characterized by a deep, squarish, rather wide channel running along the suture. Periostracum heavy, felt-like and grey. The squarish shoulder is weakly beaded in the earlier whorls. Fairly common in shallow water from Cape Cod to northeastern Florida. Introduced to California prior to 1948.

Channeled Whelk
6 in (15 cm)

Harford's Spindle, *Fusinus harfordi* (Stearns, 1871). Shell of moderate size, fusiform, solid with a white aperture half the length of the shell. Exterior dark, orange-brown, with eleven or twelve wide, rounded ribs crossed by small, sharply raised, fine, scaled spiral cords. Inside of aperture with numerous, weak, white, spiral lirae. Siphonal canal moderately long. This genus belongs in the family Fasciolariidae. The species is uncommon off British Columbia to northern California.

Harford's Spindle
2 in (5 cm)

Nassa Mud Snails
(*Family Nassariidae*)

These small sand- and mud-dwelling snails are common scavengers in most parts of the world, particularly in warm seas where there are large stretches of sand and mud flats left exposed at low tide. The operculum is chitinous, oval and usually with a serrated edge.

Eastern Mud Snail, *Ilyanassa obsoleta* (Say, 1822). A gregarious, abundant species on intertidal mud flats. Shell ovate, solid, smoothish with a high, slightly convex spire. Aperture one third the length of the shell. Colour dark-brown with a narrow, tan, colour band on the middle of the last whorl. Aperture chocolate-brown. Columella with a strong spiral tooth at the base. Ranges from Quebec to northeast Florida; introduced to British Columbia and California.

Eastern Mud Snail
0.8 in (2 cm)

Giant Western Nassa, *Nassarius fossatus* (Gould, 1849). One of the largest known nassas. Orange-brown to grey in colour. Early whorls coarsely beaded; last whorl with about a dozen coarse, variously sized, flat-topped spiral threads and short axial riblets. A common intertidal species from Vancouver Island to Mexico.

Giant Western Nassa
1.5 in (4 cm)

Western Lean Nassa, *Nassarius mendicus* (Gould, 1849). Spire high. Sculpture of numerous, small beads. Common in shallow water from Alaska to California.

Western Lean Nassa
0.8 in (2 cm)

Western Fat Nassa, *Nassarius perpinquis* (Hinds, 1844). Fairly thin-shelled but strong, with a straight, acute spire and an aperture less than half the length of the shell. Outer lip fragile. Characterized by a neat beaded sculpture. Parietal wall glazed over with tan, while the remainder of the shell is yellowish brown. There is a small white tooth on the upper part of the inner wall. Columella arched and ending below with a single, spiral lira. Inside of outer lip with fine lirae. Abundant on intertidal flats to a depth of 330 ft (100 m) from Vancouver Island to Baja California.

Western Fat Nassa
1 in (2.5 cm)

Pygmy Nassa, *Nassarius pygmaeus* (Lamarck, 1822). Shell small, with an acute spire, swollen last whorl, strongly sculptured with axial ribs bearing round beads. Aperture small, ovate and encircled with a thick, beaded outer lip and arched, glossy columella. Base of columella with two whitish swellings. Nine or ten small teeth within the outer lip. Siphonal canal wide and with a gutter above it on the last whorl. Colour brownish grey, sometimes with three subdued spiral bands. Uncommon just offshore to 655 ft (200 m) on sandy bottoms. Ranges from southern Norway, the Shetlands to the British Isles. Some workers place it in the genus, or subgenus, *Hinia*.

Pygmy Nassa
0.5 in (1.2 cm)

New England Nassa, *Nassarius trivittatus* (Say, 1822). Rather light-shelled, with eight or nine whorls which are slightly channeled below the suture. Apex acute. Spiral sculpture of four or five rows of strong, distinct beads. Parietal wall glazed with white enamel. Outer lip sharp and thin. Colour yellowish grey. Lives in shallow water down to 230 ft (70 m) on sand. Common from Newfoundland to off northeast Florida.

New England Nassa
0.7 in (2 cm)

Common Eastern Nassa, *Nassarius vibex* (Say, 1822). Shell small, but solid, with a well-developed parietal shield. Last whorl with about a dozen, poorly-developed, axial ribs which are coarsely beaded. Colour grey-brown to whitish with a few blotches or broken bands of darker brown. Inside of outer lip with four or five enamel teeth, the largest at the top. Siphonal canal recurved; columella with two small spiral lirae at the base. Parietal shield sometimes yellowish. A common intertidal mudflat species ranging from southern Cape Cod to Florida, Texas and to Brazil.

Common Eastern Nassa
0.5 in (1.2 cm)

Thickened Nassa, *Nassarius incrassatus* (Ström, 1768). A small, thick shell with an acute spire and small aperture surrounded by a thickened lip. Five whorls with ten to twelve rounded axial ribs crossed by numerous spiral ridges. Suture wavy. Parietal shield and outer lip enamel-white. Behind the lip is a swollen varix. Inside of outer lip with five or six small lirae. Colour reddish buff to yellow-grey,

Thickened Nassa
0.5 in (1.2 cm)

sometimes with a subsutural darker band. Common in large colonies in muddy areas. Its range extends from most of western Europe into the Mediterranean. Belongs to the subgenus *Tritonella*.

Reticulated Nassa, *Nassarius reticulatus* (Linnaeus, 1758). Solid, heavy, coarse shell, quite variable in its sculpturing which may be coarsely beaded or with widely spaced, coarsely knobbed axial ribs. Suture well-indented and usually with a row of separate beads below it. Parietal wall well-callused. Colour glossy-white with fine brown spiral lines and occasional dark blotches. These scavengers live in pockets of soft sand among rocky intertidal areas. The species is widely distributed from the Black Sea north to the British Isles and Norway.

Reticulated Nassa
1 in (2.5 cm)

Olive Shells
(*Family Olividae*)

Although the glossy and attractive olive shells are associated with tropical waters, there are two species that have invaded the cooler waters of the Eastern Pacific. There is no operculum in the true *Oliva*, but some smaller *Olivella* have a chitinous one. All species are carnivorous scavengers. There are no olive shells in western Europe.

Purple Dwarf Olive, *Olivella biplicata* (Sowerby, 1825). Quite solid, globular-elongate. Upper columella wall with a heavy, white callus. Lower end of columella with a raised, spiral fold which is cut by two or three spiral, incised lines. Colour bluish grey with violet stains around the fasciole and lower part of the aperture. Abundant in summer months in sandy bays and beaches. Ranges from Vancouver Island to Baja California.

Purple Dwarf Olive
1 in (2.5 cm)

Beatic Dwarf Olive, *Olivella baetica* Carpenter, 1864. Small, light-shelled, glossy and coloured a drab-tan with weak purplish brown maculations arranged in axial flames. Fasciole white, often stained with brown. A moderately common, shallow-water sand species living from Kodiak Island, Alaska, to Baja California.

Beatic Dwarf Olive
0.5 in (1.2 cm)

False Greenland Mitre, *Volutomitra groenlandica* (Moller, 1842). Fusiform, solid, white with a dark-brown periostracum. Smoothish, the nuclear whorls smooth, the others with fine, spiral scratches. Minute axial riblets on the early whorls. Columella with four folds. Operculum chitinous. Uncommon; this offshore species belongs to the family Volutomitridae.

False Greenland Mitre
1 in (2.5 cm)

Mitres and False Mitres

(*Families Mitridae and Volutomitridae*)

Both families are related, but their internal anatomy is different. The Volutomitridae are mainly cold-water dwellers, there being two from the Atlantic and one in the northwest Pacific. The Mitridae are mainly tropical. Both have two to four strong, oblique, spiral folds, or teeth, on the columella.

Alaskan False Mitre, *Volutomitra alaskana* Dall 1902. Fusiform, solid, resembling the False Greenland Mitre, but having a longer aperture and a thicker, smooth greenish brown periostracum. In both species the early whorls are badly eroded. A carnivorous species living in deep water from Pribilof Islands, Alaska, to off San Diego, California.

Alaskan False Mitre
1.5 in (4 cm)

Ebony Mitre, *Mitra ebenus* (Lamarck, 1811). Fusiform, solid, smooth, with slightly convex whorls and an indented suture. Aperture slightly more than half the length of the shell. Surface smooth, with about ten low, rounded ribs. Colour blackish brown. Upper third of the last whorl with a narrow spiral band of tan. Columella with two large and two small, slanting folds. Outer lip thickened and with tiny teeth on the inner edge. Moderately

Ebony Mitre
1.2 in (3 cm)

common in rock pools in Mediterranean and Portugal.

Little Trumpet Mitre, *Mitra cornicula* (Linnaeus, 1758). Similar to the Ebony Mitre, but with smaller, weaker columella folds, a smooth outer lip, and with about seven or eight spiral threads on the base of the shell. Lacks ribs. Colour glossy brown. A common littoral species of the Mediterranean extending to the Azores and to Portugal.

Little Trumpet Mitre
0.7 in (2 cm)

✦

Volutes and Cones

(Families Volutidae and Conidae)

These two major families are poorly represented in northern waters. Only one volute exists in the cold waters of the north Pacific, and the only volute in western Europe is the Spotted Flask. Many hundreds of cones live in the warm waters of the world, but only the Mediterranean Cone comes as far north as Portugal.

Stearns' Volute, *Arctomelon stearnsi* (Dall, 1872). Shell large, fusiform, strong; the exterior chalky-grey with mauve-brown undertones. Aperture semi-glossy and light-brown . Nuclear whorls bulbous, smooth, but often eroded away. Columella brownish and with two large folds and a third

Stearns' Volute
4 in (10 cm)

weaker one below. Locally common offshore in Alaska.

Spotted Flask, *Ampulla priamus* (Gmelin, 1791). Shell oval, thin-shelled but strong, with only three or four convex whorls. Smooth, shiny, light-brown with six distantly placed rows of small, round dots of reddish brown on the last whorl. Outer lip thin and sharp. No operculum. Frequently dredged in fairly deep water off Spain and Portugal. *Halia* is a synonym.

Spotted Flask
2.5 in (6.5 cm)

Mediterranean Cone, *Conus ventricosus* (Gmelin, 1791) . Shell elongate-conic, solid, with a short, flattish spire and straight sides, with weak spiral incised lines at the base. Colour variable, but usually a dull-brown or maculated or with a light spiral band at the middle. Base of the outer lip with a brown edge. A common Mediterranean shallow-water cone also found in Portugal.

Mediterranean Cone
1 in (2.5 cm)

Turrids
(Family Turridae)

This is a very large, worldwide family with hundreds of genera and thousands of species, thus making it a difficult group to identify without extensive, well-illustrated monographs. Most are fusiform and rather small, with a slit, notch or U-shaped canal at the top of the outer lip, known as the "turrid" notch. Operculum chitinous.

Slender Mangelia, *Mangelia gracilis* (Montagu, 1803). Shell evenly fusiform, with a high, acute spire. Whorls nine, bearing ten to fourteen rounded axial ribs which are on the upper third of the last whorl. Spiral sculpture of minute threads overriding the ribs. Outer lip sharp, thickened behind by a swollen varix, and with a small, but deep "turrid" notch. Colour cream with yellow banding. Occurs on gravel bottoms from 23 to 492 ft (7–150 m) from the Mediterranean to the southern British Isles.

Slender Mangelia
0.8 in (2 cm)

Incised Drillia, *Ophiodermella incisa* (Carpenter, 1865). Fusiform, solid; covered with numerous, spiral cut lines. "Turrid notch" very shallow and weak. Periostracum brownish. Operculum chitinous with a terminal nucleus. Common offshore from Puget Sound to California.

Incised Drillia
0.5 in (1.2 cm)

Goode's Aforia, *Aforia goodei* (Dall, 1890). Shell fairly large, light-weight, fusiform and chalky white. There is a strong, spiral cord on the shoulder of the whorls. Above it are axial growth scars showing the former "turrid notches." Common from off British Columbia to southern Chile.

Goode's Aforia
3.5 in (9 cm)

✦

Bubble Shells
(*Families Acteonidae and Scaphandridae*)

The great snail subclass Opisthobranchia contains a vast number of diverse hermaphrodites that includes the naked seaslugs, or nudibranchs, and the bubble shells with their very delicate, coiled shells. Most lack an operculum, with the exception of *Acteon*.

Lathe Acteon, *Acteon tornatilis* (Linnaeus, 1758). Shell broadly fusiform, solid, with a convex spire and long aperture three-quarters the length of the entire shell. Sculpture of numerous, very fine, spiral incised lines becoming stronger towards the base of the shell. Colour pinkish yellow with three lighter spiral bands, two being bordered by a dark-brown line. Operculum chitinous. Occurs offshore from Iceland to Spain.

Lathe Acteon
0.5 in (1.2 cm)

Giant Canoe-bubble, *Scaphander punctostriatus* Mighels, 1841. Shell light-weight, ovate-oblong. Apex with a slightly sunken area. Aperture constricted above, the outer lip projecting above the apex. Shell smoothish, except for numerous, spiral rows of microscopic, elongate punctations. Colour chalk-white, with a straw periostracum. Moderately common offshore on sand. Ranges

Giant Canoe-bubble
1.5 in (3.5 cm)

from the Arctic Seas to Florida; Greenland and Iceland, uncommon.

Wooden Canoe-bubble, *Scaphander lignarius* (Linnaeus, 1758). Shell solid, opaque, ovate-oblong, with the upper half constricted. Exterior cream, with numerous, fine spiral scratches and brown lines. Colour variable from yellow to brownish green. A common sublittoral sand-dwelling species. It ranges from the British Isles to the Mediterranean and the Canary Islands.

Wooden Canoe-bubble
1 in (2.5 cm)

Open Paper-bubble, *Philine aperta* (Linnaeus, 1767). Shell fragile, translucent, oval, with a very large, wide aperture. Outer lip projects above the apex. Pale-yellow animal covers the shell. The skin is capable of secreting a protective layer of sulphuric acid. Within the stomach of all *Philine* are three solid, flat gizzard plates. It lives on sandy bottoms and preys upon small molluscs and polychaete worms. This is a common offshore species ranging from Norway to the Mediterranean, as well as South Africa and the Indian Ocean.

Open Paper-bubble
1.5 in (4 cm)

Gould's Paper-bubble, *Haminoea vesicula* Gould, 1855. Shell very fragile, globular, translucent yellow, with a thin rusty brown or yellowish orange periostracum. There is a very small perforation at the concealed apex. Similar to *H. virescens*, but the body whorl is larger, the aperture smaller and the columella thickened at the base and forming

Gould's Paper-bubble
0.7 in (2 cm)

an indented umbilicus. Belongs in the family Haminoeidae. A common, littoral bay species ranging from southern Alaska to the Gulf of California.

Sowerby's Paper-bubble, *Haminoea virescens* (Sowerby, 1833). Shell, fragile, globular and translucent greenish yellow in colour. Aperture very large and open. Upper part of the outer lip high and narrowly winged. No apical hole. The animal is dark-green with yellowish markings: dots on the head shield, mottlings on the parapodia. A common, shallow-water species of the open coast. It prefers sandy areas where there are beds of seagrass where it lays small gelatinous egg masses on the stems of weeds. Found from Puget Sound, Washington, to the Gulf of California.

Sowerby's Paper-bubble
0.5 in (1.2 cm)

Solitary Paper-bubble, *Haminoea solitaria* (Say, 1822). Shell fragile, oblong, with the aperture as long as the entire shell. Apertural lip arising on the right side of the apical perforation. Spiral sculpture of numerous, very fine scratches. Colour translucent amber to whitish. Prefers a shallow sandy area where there are protective grasses. It lays its gelatinous egg masses on the stems of weeds. This is a common, carnivorous species distributed from Cape Cod, Massachusetts, to off North Carolina.

Solitary Paper-bubble
0.5 in (1.2 cm)

Watery Paper-bubble, *Haminoea hydatis* (Linnaeus, 1758). Shell fragile, globular, inflated, translucent white or yellowish, with the aperture slightly longer than the spire. Columella thickened with a white glaze. Exterior surface smooth, except for fine, irregular growth lines. Soft parts light-brown and cover most of the shell. The anterior cephalic disc bears two small black eyes on the dorsal surface. This species feeds on small bivalves. It occurs in muddy sand in subtidal areas from the British Isles to the Mediterranean.

Watery Paper-bubble
0.5 in (1.2 cm)

Bubble Akera, *Akera bullata* Müller, 1776. Shell fragile, globular and the whorls enrolled at the apex. The shell is carried externally at the hind end of an elongate animal which has two elongate parapodia extending over the back of the animal and part of the shell. Lacks tentacles. Soft parts pale-grey to orange, with many small white and black spots and streaks. A purple fluid may be secreted if the animal is disturbed. It is capable of swimming by flapping its parapodia. This carnivore lives in sandy and weedy areas and serves as a food for flounders. It ranges from Norway, throughout the British Isles, south into the Mediterranean.

Bubble Akera
0.7 in (2 cm)

✦

Sea Butterflies (*Order Pteropoda*)

The world's oceans are heavily populated with these small, abundant snails that live near the surface and form a large part of the planktonic hordes upon which most life in the seas depends, particularly some species of whales and oceanic fishes. The shells are delicate, glassy and translucent. There are fifteen genera and about a hundred species, most with a worldwide distribution in both cold and warm seas.

Uncinate Cavoline, *Cavolinia uncinata* (Rang, 1829). Shell small, glassy, translucent and brownish. Dorsal lip with a thin margin. Ventral lip not more developed than the dorsal one. Shell with distinct lateral points. Upper lip flattened posteriorly. This is usually a warm-water, pelagic species found in the Atlantic as far north as Newfoundland and Alaska. There are five common species in this genus.

Uncinate Cavoline
0.5 in (1.2 cm)

Pyramid Clio, *Clio pyramidata* Linnaeus, 1767. Shell of an angular form, compressed, colourless and with lateral keels. A cross-section of the front end is always angular at the sides. There is usually a ridge extending longitudinally along the back. Surface with wavy ribs. A worldwide pelagic species and popular food of whales.

Pyramid Clio
0.7 in (2 cm)

Cigar Pteropod, *Cuvierina columnella* (Rang, 1827). Shell small, cylindrical, shaped somewhat like a fat cigar. Surface smooth. A cross-section is almost circular. Behind the aperture there is a slight constriction. This is the only species in the genus.

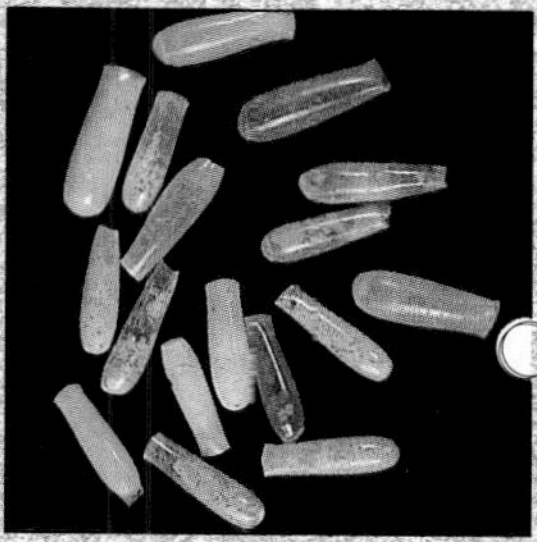

Cigar Pteropod
0.4 in (1 cm)

✦

TUSK
SHELLS

Tusk Shells

(*Class Scaphopoda*)

This group of sand-dwelling molluscs is worldwide in distribution, but has fewer than a thousand species. The shell is open at both ends. The narrow end protrudes above the sandy bottom where water is drawn in and expelled at alternating intervals. At the large end, the conic-shaped foot and dozens of ciliated, prehensile threads project through the sand. Tusk shells feed upon single-celled foraminifera. Identification depends upon the nature of the slits at the small end of the shell and in the nature of the ribbing.

Wampum Tusk, *Antalis pretiosum* (Sowerby, 1860). Moderately curved and solid; opaque-white, ivory-like, commonly with faint dirty-yellow rings of growth. Apex with a short notch on the convex side. A common offshore species living in sandy mud. It was used extensively as money by the northwest Indian tribes. It ranges from Alaska to Baja California.

Wampum Tusk
2 in (5 cm)

Western Straight Tusk, *Laevidentalium rectius* (Carpenter, 1864). Almost straight, slender and long and attenuated towards the apex. Thin-shelled and fragile. Surface glossy and smoothish. Colour bluish white, somewhat translucent, with some opaque-white flecks and rings. Apical opening without a notch. Moderately common offshore from Alaska to Panama.

Western Straight Tusk
1.2 in (3 cm)

Western Atlantic Tusk, *Antalis occidentale* (Stimpson, 1851). Sixteen to eighteen primary ribs, fairly distinct in the young stages. Sculptureless in the senile stage. Round in cross-section. Common offshore from Newfoundland to off North Carolina.

Western Atlantic Tusk
1.2 in (3 cm)

Entale Tusk, *Antalis entalis* (Linnaeus, 1758). Moderately curved, solid, round in cross-section and finely striate longitudinally. Colour ivory-white, sometimes with a rusty stain on the narrow end, caused by a mixture of mud and sand in which it burrows. Margin of larger end often jagged. Small end with a very short, oblique pipe or tubular appendage having a pear-shaped opening. This is a common, sand-dwelling, offshore species found in Arctic waters from Nova Scotia to Massachusetts; and from Iceland and Norway south to off Portugal.

Entale Tusk
2 in (5 cm)

Common Tusk, *Antalis vulgaris* (da Costa, 1778). Moderately curved, solid and wide. Circular in cross-section. Opaque-white, sometimes tinted with yellowish brown or rose towards the narrow, apical end. Sculpture of fine, crowded longitudinal striae, about thirty at the apex. Aperture oblique, thin and jagged. Anal opening small, round or ovate and occupying a very short tube. No notch or slit present. Common offshore in muddy and sandy areas from southern England and Ireland southward into the Mediterranean.

Common Tusk
2 in (5 cm)

European Tusk, *Dentalium dentale* Linnaeus, 1766. Moderately curved, rather slender. Opaque-white, sometimes suffused with rose at the smaller end. Sculpture of about ten strong, rounded, longitudinal ribs near the apex, becoming eighteen to twenty near the aperture. Aperture rounded, polygonal, slightly oblique. Anal orifice small, circular and with very thick walls. No notch or slit present. This is a southern species living offshore from Portugal south into the Mediterranean and the Adriatic.

European Tusk
1 in (2.5 cm)

✦

THE CHITONS

Chitons
(*Class Polyplacophora*)

These rock-dwelling, elongate molluscs have eight shelly plates bound together at the sides by a leathery girdle which may be smooth, hairy or covered with small, shelly scales. The flat foot occupies most of the underside, with the small head possessing a mouth with radular teeth, but without tentacles or eyes. There are about 600 species throughout the world.

Northern Red Chiton, *Tonicella rubra* (Linnaeus, 1767). Oblong, moderately elevated, and with the valves rather rounded. Upper surfaces smooth, except for fine growth wrinkles. Coloured light-tan over which are orange-red marblings. Interior of valves bright pink. Girdle reddish brown, covered with minute, elongate, separate scales. Common on hard surfaces from 9 to 656 ft (3–200 m). Arctic Seas to Connecticut; also Bering Strait to northern California; Norway to Portugal.

Northern Red Chiton
1 in (2.5 cm)

Mottled Red Chiton, *Tonicella marmorea* (Fabricius, 1780). Oblong to oval, elevated, and rather sharply angular. Upper surface smoothish and with microscopic granulations. Interior of valves tinted with rose. Girdle leathery and without scales or bristles. Common from 9 to 328 ft (3–100 m). Greenland to Massachusetts; Japan and Alaska to Washington State; Norway to the British Isles.

Mottled Red Chiton
1 in (2.5 cm)

Lined Red Chiton, *Tonicella lineata* (Wood, 1815). Valves shiny smooth, orange to deep-red with oblique black lines bordered with white. Interior of valves white. Girdle naked. Common in shallow water from Japan to Alaska to northern California.

Lined Red Chiton
1.2 in (3 cm)

Mertens' Chiton, *Lepidozona mertensii* (Middendorff, 1847). Oval in shape; colour variable: commonly yellowish with dark reddish brown streaks and maculations. Central areas of the valves with strong, longitudinal ribs and smaller, cross ridges which give a netted appearance. Anterior valve with thirty or more radial rows of tiny warts. Interior of valves whitish. Girdle with alternating yellow and reddish bands, and covered with tiny, low, smooth, split-pea scales. Abundant in shallow water on hard surfaces. Ranges from the Aleutian Islands to Baja California, Mexico.

Mertens' Chiton
1.5 in (4 cm)

Mossy Mopalia, *Mopalia muscosa* (Gould, 1846). Oblong to oval. Head valve with ten beaded ribs. Colour usually a dull-brown, blackish olive or greyish. Interior of valves blue-green, rarely stained pinkish. Girdle with stiff hairs resembling a fringe of moss. Many varieties were described. This is a common intertidal species ranging along the entire coast from Alaska to Baja California, Mexico.

Mossy Mopalia
1.5 in (4 cm)

Eastern American Chiton, *Chaetopleura apiculata* (Say, 1830). Small, oblong to oval. Valves slightly carinate. Central area of valves with fifteen to twenty longitudinal rows of raised, neat beads. Lateral areas distinctly defined, raised, and bearing numerous, larger beads. Interior of valves white or greyish. Girdle narrow, mottled cream and brown, and microscopically granulose and sparsely scattered with short, transparent hairs. This common species is usually found attached to small rocks and to dead shells in shallow water. It ranges from Cape Cod, Massachusetts, to both sides of Florida.

Eastern American Chiton
0.8 in (2 cm)

THE
BIVALVES

The Bivalves
(*Class Bivalvia*)

The class Bivalvia or Pelecypoda includes such molluscs as the clams, oysters and scallops. There are about 10,000 living species, most living in the world's seas, but many are found only in freshwater rivers and lakes. The soft parts lack a true head and radular teeth, and are protected by two shelly valves, hence the name "bivalves". Locomotion is accomplished by a tongue-like foot that protrudes from the front end. Some species, like the oysters, become permanently attached to the substrate. At the rear are two fleshy, tube-like siphons, sometimes fused into one, through which water is inhaled or exhaled. Microscopic forms of vegetable matter are drawn in over the mucus-covered gills and passed into a small mouth. In most clams the sexes are in separate individuals, but a few are hermaphroditic or can change sex periodically. Eggs are sometimes brooded within the gills or may be shed into the open sea where released sperm can fertilize them. The larval or veliger forms of bivalves float and swim freely, sometimes for many kilometres before they settle down on the bottom and change into shelly bivalves. Bivalves may have a life span of two to one hundred years.

The valves of bivalves are held together by one or two adductor muscles, and are kept ajar by a chitinous, elastic ligament which may sometimes be located internally between the teeth of the hinge. The shape and number of hinge teeth, the outline of the muscle scars on the inside of the valves, and the exterior sculpturing are used in identifying the various species.

Awning Clams
(*Family Solemyacidae*)

This is a relatively obscure and primitive-looking group of bivalves living in mud in U-shaped burrows that are open at each end. The oblong, cigar-shaped shells lack hinge teeth and are covered with a glossy, thin, brown periostracum which extends well beyond the margins of the shell. The foot is large and sucker-like at the broadened, flat end. The short siphonal opening is bordered by fleshy, tentacle-like appendages. The ligament is internal and near the posterior beak end. These clams harbour symbiotic bacteria to reduce sulphur oxides. The family appears to be absent in northwestern Europe.

Boreal Awning Clam, *Solemya borealis* Totten, 1834. Shell fragile, oblong, somewhat compressed laterally and with a glossy, rayed, chestnut-brown periostracum. Interior of valves greyish blue. Siphonal opening with three pairs of long tentacles on the upper part, and fifteen smaller ones bordering the lower half. Moderately common offshore from Nova Scotia to Connecticut.

Boreal Awning Clam
2.5 in (6.5 cm)

Atlantic Awning Clam, *Solemya velum* Say, 1822. Shell small; periostracum glossy light-brown with lighter radial rays of yellowish. Chondrophore supported by two curved arms. Siphonal opening with two pairs of small tubercles above, and five or six pairs of short tentacles below. A common, shallow-water species

Atlantic Awning Clam
1 in (2.5 cm)

ranging from Nova Scotia to northern Florida.

Toga Awning Clam, *Solemya togata* (Poli, 1795). Shell fragile; periostracum reddish brown with lighter rays. Offshore in mud from Portugal to West Africa and the Mediterranean.

Toga Awning Clam
2 in (5 cm)

✦

Nut Clams
(*Family Nuculidae*)

These small clams have been abundant since the earliest development of bivalves during the Ordovician, 500 million years ago. They are characterized by their pearly interior and numerous, small "taxodont" teeth in the hinge. Below the beaks is a chitinous resilium set in a cup, or chondrophore. There is no pallial sinus scar. The shell's edge is crenulated in some species. Nut clams are distributed worldwide and are well-represented in cold waters, serving as food for bottom fish.

Atlantic Nut Clam, *Nucula proxima* Say, 1822. Very small, solid, obliquely ovate, smooth. Colour greenish grey with microscopic, embedded, axial, grey lines and prominent, irregular, brownish, concentric rings. Outer shell overcast with an oily iridescence. Ventral edge minutely crenulate. A common, shallow-water species found in

Atlantic Nut Clam
0.3 in (7 mm)

sand and mud. Ranges from Nova Scotia to Florida and to Texas.

Smooth Nut Clam, *Nucula tenuis* (Montagu, 1808). Shell very small, ovate, smooth, except for irregular growth lines. Colour a shiny, olive-green, sometimes with darker lines of growth. No radial lines present. Ventral edge smooth. Moderately common offshore in Arctic Seas, south to Florida; south to Spain; Japan to Alaska and south to California.

Smooth Nut Clam
0.2 in (5 mm)

Nuclear Nut Clam, *Nucula nucleus* (Linnaeus, 1758). Shell small, ovate; beaks behind midline; triangular in outline. Ventral edge crenulate. Common offshore from Norway to Africa; Labrador to Florida; Alaska to Mexico.

Nuclear Nut Clam
0.4 in (1 cm)

✦

Pointed Nut Clams
(*Family Nuculanidae*)

These nut clams have a porcellaneous, rather than pearly, shell, and are usually rather drawn out or pointed at the posterior end. The chondrophore cup between the rows of taxodont teeth is usually rather large. The shells may have a prominent and deep pallial sinus. Most of these clams live offshore in cold waters.

Pointed Nut Clam, *Nuculana acuta* (Conrad, 1831). Shell very small, solid, rounded at the front end, pointed at the rear. Apex of the pallial sinus is broadly U-shaped. Concentric ribs evenly sized and evenly spaced extend over the rib which borders the dorsal surface of the pointed end. Colour white with a thin, yellowish periostracum. This is a common, shallow-water species ranging from Cape Cod to Brazil.

Pointed Nut Clam
0.3 in (7 mm)

Fossa Nut Clam, *Nuculana fossa* (Baird, 1863). Shell elongate, moderately fat and smoothish, except for small, pronounced, concentric ribs at the anterior end and on the beaks. Dorsal area of rostrum is smoothish, depressed and bounded by two weak radial ribs. Found in sand at 3 to 459 ft (1–140 m) from Alaska to Puget Sound, Washington .

Fossa Nut Clam
1 in (2.5 cm)

Almond Yoldia, *Yoldia amygdalea* Valenciennes, 1846. Shell thin, compressed laterally, elongate and narrowing at the posterior end. The anterior ventral margin has a small concave depression. Moderately common in Arctic Seas to California, the Gulf of Maine, and to Norway.

Almond Yoldia
2 in (5 cm)

✦

Ark Clams
(*Family Arcidae*)

Ark shells are distributed in most warm-water seas around the world, with only a few extending into cooler waters. The oblong, sturdy shells are characterized by a straight hinge bearing many, small, interlocking "taxodont" teeth. In the true arks, there is a natural gape in the ventral edge of the shell through which passes the foot that spins a strong cluster of byssal threads.

Four-sided Ark, *Arca tetragona* Poli, 1795. Shell solid, box-shaped, with the widely separated beaks in the front half of the shell. There is a wide ventral gape where the massive, green byssus protrudes. Exterior finely reticulated and dirty white to yellowish with a brown periostracum. Ligament in a number of grooves radiating from the beaks across the cardinal area. Hinge plate straight, with forty to fifty small, similar teeth. Common in shallow water from Norway to the Mediterranean and Azores.

Four-sided Ark
1.3 in (3 cm)

Transverse Ark, *Anadara transversa* (Say, 1822). Shell solid, quadrate-oval; left valve overlaps the right valve. Thirty to thirty-five ribs per valve, those on the left valve usually beaded. Ligament long, narrow and pustulose. Fairly common in mud below low tide mark. Ranges from Cape Cod to Florida and to Texas.

Transverse Ark
1 in (2.5 cm)

Blood Ark, *Anadara ovalis* (Bruguière, 1789). Shell fat and oval, white, with twenty-six to thirty-five smooth ribs. Ligament very narrow and depressed; beaks close together. Periostracum blackish brown, hairy and fairly thick. Flesh and blood are red. A common shallow-water ark found from Cape Cod to Texas.

Blood Ark
2 in (5 cm)

Milky Ark, *Arcopsis lactea* (Linnaeus, 1767). Shell small, solid, rhomboidal in outline; somewhat compressed. Beaks just in front of the mid-line and far apart. Hinge plate with forty to fifty small teeth. Exterior yellowish white, with a light-brown periostracum, sometimes overhanging the margins. Sculpture of fine radiating ribs crossed by concentric ridges. Interior whitish; muscle scars raised. A common intertidal species attached to rocks in sandy areas. Ranges from the southern coast of Britain to the Mediterranean and to South Africa.

Milky Ark
0.5 in (1.2 cm)

Nodulose Ark, *Acar nodulosa* (Müller, 1776). Shell small, solid, elongate-rhomboidal, with a narrower front end and a broader, spathate hind end. Beaks nearer the smaller front end and set slightly apart. Ligament long, narrow and arrow-shaped. Hinge with about seven teeth in front, and about twelve slanting ones at the posterior end. Sculpture of worn reticulation and beads. Periostracum thin and light-brown. Interior of valves white. Byssal gape very small. A common

Nodulose Ark
0.5 in (1.2 cm)

offshore and deepwater species ranging from Norway to Portugal.

Sulcate Limopsis, *Limopsis sulcata* Verrill and Bush, 1898. Shell small, obliquely oval, with prominent, rounded ribs which are finely cut on the upper edge by short, radial grooves. Inner margin of the valves smooth. Colour dull-white. Periostracum thick, tufted, extending beyond the ventral edge of the shell. Hinge arched, with about six small teeth on either side of the centre. Ligament external, small, central and triangular. Moderately common in sand offshore to a depth of about 2,296 ft (700 m). Ranges from Cape Cod to Texas and the West Indies. Belongs to the family Limopsidae.

Sulcate Limopsis
0.5 in (1.2 cm)

✦

Bittersweet Clams and Date Mussels

(*Families Glycymerididae and Mytilidae*)

The sturdy, oval, bittersweet clams of the family Glycymerididae have an arched hinge with a few taxodont teeth. The exterior is either smooth or strongly ribbed. Among the family Mytilidae are several species of date mussels that are adapted for boring by means of carbonic acid and shell rotation.

West Coast Bittersweet, *Glycymeris subobsoleta* (Carpenter, 1864). Shell solid, compressed laterally, slightly longer than high, and chalky white with brownish markings. Periostracum velvety, but usually worn away. Radial ribs, flat with narrow interspaces. About nine short, elongate teeth on either side of the centre of the hinge. Ventral edge with white teeth and brown colouring between. Moderately common just offshore to 26 ft (8 m) from the Aleutians to southern California.

West Coast Bittersweet
1 in (2.5 cm)

European Bittersweet, *Glycymeris glycymeris* (Linnaeus, 1758). Shell solid, beaks central; almost circular in outline. Colour yellow-brown, sometimes with irregular zigzag patterns. With very fine concentric and radiating lines. Very common offshore to 229 ft (70 m) on sandy gravel bottoms from Norway to the Mediterranean and Canary Islands.

European Bittersweet
2.5 in (6 cm)

European Date Mussel, *Lithophaga lithophaga* (Linnaeus, 1758). Elongate, cigar-shaped. Umbo at the narrow anterior end. Exterior light-brown with fine growth lines. Interior bluish white. No hinge teeth. Bores in shallow-water rocks. Portugal to the Mediterranean and Adriatic Seas.

European Date Mussel
2.7 in (7 cm)

Mussels
(*Family Mytilidae*)

The mussel family is quite diverse, with many genera and species, some of which have been accidentally introduced around the world on ships' bottoms and floating logs. Mussels become attached to hard substrates by means of a multi-threaded byssus spun by a short foot. A few species burrow into peat, rocks and coral. Many are an important food for man, especially in France and Japan.

Blue Mussel, *Mytilus edulis* Linnaeus, 1758. Shell spathate, with the umbones at the narrow end. Ventral margin often curved. Colour blue-black with eroded areas of chalky purple. Periostracum varnish-like. Interior pearly white with a deep-blue border. Occasionally specimens have rays of brownish yellow. Occurs in large numbers attached to intertidal rocks in the lower Arctic Ocean south to South Carolina; south to California; and in western Europe south to the Black Sea.

Blue Mussel
2.5 in (6 cm)

Mediterranean Blue Mussel, *Mytilus galloprovincialis* Lamarck, 1822. Similar to the Blue Mussel, but is usually larger, broader, and more angular. The mantle edge of the animal is blue-black, whereas in *edulis* it is straw-coloured. Periostracum dark and shiny. A common intertidal species farmed in western Europe.

Mediterranean Blue Mussel
4 in (10 cm)

Californian Mussel, *Mytilus californianus* Conrad, 1837. Shell large, thick, inflated. Ventral margin straight, with a dozen weak radial ribs and coarse growth lines. Abundant intertidally from the Aleutians to north west Mexico.

Californian Mussel
5 in (12.5 cm)

Falcate Date Mussel, *Adula falcata* (Gould, 1851). Very elongate, cylindrical, slightly curved. Beaks rounded and about one eighth the length from the swollen anterior end. A strong angular rib runs from the beaks to the base of the posterior end. Sculpture of numerous vertical, wavy and slightly beaded ribs is present over the entire shell. Colour shiny chestnut-brown. A fairly common rock-borer in shallow water from Coos Bay, Oregon, south to Mexico.

Falcate Date Mussel
3 in (7.5 cm)

Californian Date Mussel, *Adula californiensis* (Philippi, 1847). Similar to the Falcate Date Mussel, but chubbier, not as elongate and has a smooth surface. A velvety, hair-like periostracum covers the compressed posterior end. Colour a shiny chocolate-brown. It makes burrows in hard rocks in shallow water. Moderately common from British Columbia to southern California.

California Date Mussel
1 in (2.5 cm)

Hooked Mussel, *Ischadium recurvum* (Rafinesque, 1820). Flattish, rather wide, with numerous wavy axial ribs. Colour of exterior dark greyish brown; inside purplish to rosy brown with a narrow blue-grey border. Three or four small teeth at the edge of the posterior end. A common

Hooked Mussel
1.5 in (4 cm)

brackish water rock-dweller living from Cape Cod to the West Indies.

Senhouse's Mussel
1 in (2.5 cm)

Senhouse's Mussel, *Muscilista senhousei* (Benson, 1842). Shell small, rather fragile, thin-shelled and coloured green to bluish green with delicate, zigzag brownish flames. Ends with fine radiating striae. Lunule with a crenulated margin. Common; makes nests on mud flats and attaches to wooden pilings. Introduced from Asia to Washington to central California.

Northern Horse Mussel
4 in (10 cm)

Northern Horse Mussel, *Modiolus modiolus* (Linnaeus, 1758). Shell strong, oblong, swollen, with a coarse, rather thick blackish brown periostracum with long, smooth hairs. Beaks always white and not swollen. Adult shells chalky, mauve-white. No hinge teeth. A common, circumpolar, subtidal mussel found as far south as New Jersey, central California and south to France.

Fan-shaped Horse Mussel
5 in (12.5 cm)

Fan-shaped Horse Mussel, *Modiolus rectus* (Conrad, 1837). Rectangular, well-inflated and thin-shelled. Colour bluish white with a yellowish brown periostracum. Exterior with fine growth lines. Interior pearly white, tinged with pink. Lives burrowed in mud with the broad margin exposed. In 3 to 147 ft (1–45 m) of water from British Columbia to Mexico.

Bearded Horse Mussel, *Modiolus barbatus* (Linnaeus, 1758). Shell broad at one end, somewhat compressed, and coloured yellow and reddish. Covered with a thick, yellow-brown, hairy periostracum. Interior lustrous, very pale-blue, tinted with pink. Margins smooth. Lives among rocks from low tide mark to 328 ft (100 m). Common from southern British Isles to the Mediterranean.

Bearded Horse Mussel
1 in (2.5 cm)

Adriatic Horse Mussel, *Modiolus adriaticus* Lamarck, 1822. Shell small, brittle, swollen, and with the beaks a short distance from the anterior end. Colour yellow with reddish rays or irregular zigzag streaks. Interior pearly white, with the external rays showing through. Found offshore to 262 ft (80 m) from the British Isles to the Mediterranean.

Adriatic Horse Mussel
1.5 in (4 cm)

Scallops
(*Family Pectinidae*)

The well-known, edible scallops are worldwide in distribution and contain hundreds of species divided into about fifty genera. St. James' Scallop has long been a religious symbol and extensively used in heraldry and art design.

Great Scallop, *Pecten maximus* (Linnaeus, 1758). Shell solid and circular in outline; ears equal; the right (lower) valve is quite convex and slightly overlaps the flat left (upper) valve. Upper valve with fifteen to seventeen broad, radiating ribs and coloured red-

Great Scallop
4 in (10 cm)

brown. Bottom valve white to cream with tints of yellow and pink. Common in sandy areas offshore from 3 to 393 ft (1–120 m). Distributed from Norway south to Portugal.

Giant Pacific Scallop, *Pecten caurinus* Gould, 1850. Shell large, circular in outline. The upper (left) valve is almost flat, reddish grey and with about seventeen low, rounded ribs; lower valve moderately deep, whitish and with a few more, stronger, rather flat-topped ribs. This is a popular commercial species found offshore from the Aleutians to northern California.

Giant Pacific Scallop
7 in (17.5 cm)

Atlantic Deepsea Scallop, *Placopecten magellanicus* (Gmelin, 1791). Shell large, almost circular, light-weight but strong. Both valves flattish to slightly convex. Exterior rough with numerous, very small, raised threads. Colour variable from grey to dirty-white and sometimes rayed with purplish red. Ears unequal. Common offshore. A commercial species ranging from the Maritime Provinces of Canada to off North Carolina.

Atlantic Deepsea Scallop
7 in (17.5 cm)

Hyaline Scallop, *Lissopecten hyalinus* (Poli, 1795). Shell thin, fragile, flattish, almost circular in outline, glassy, translucent golden-brown. Right (lower) valve with about five or six very weak, low ribs. Upper valve with radially cut lines. Posterior ear where the byssus emerges has about seven rough riblets. Lower margin of the byssal notch with minute teeth. A

Hyaline Scallop
1 in (2.5 cm)

shallow-water species ranging from the Adriatic and Mediterranean north to western Portugal.

Seven-rayed Scallop, *Pseudamussium septemradiatum* (Müller, 1776). Shell brittle, almost circular in outline; ears about the same size and with four to six riblets. Valves with five to eight low, rounded ribs which increase in width towards the margins. Surface with numerous radiating scratches, crossed by concentric lines. Colour of left valve brick-red or purplish brown; right valve whitish with some brick-red near the umbones. Rarely all-white. A common offshore scallop in 39 to 656 ft (12–200 m) around the British Isles. Extends from Norway to northwest Africa.

Seven-rayed Scallop
1.5 in (4 cm)

Bald Scallop, *Proteopecten glaber* (Linnaeus, 1758). Shell solid, both valves about the same thickness and with the ears about the same size. Right (lower) valve with ten or eleven raised riblets; left valve with six or seven weaker, low ribs. Ears with fine riblets. Colour variable and usually bright. Moderately common offshore from Portugal to the Mediterranean.

Bald Scallop
2 in (5 cm)

Kitten Scallop, *Camptonectes tiaerinus* (Müller, 1776). Shell small, fan-shaped, almost equivalve, and with the anterior ears about three times as long as the posterior ones. Colours and patterns variable: white, cream, grey, brown and purple, with spots, streaks and maculations. Ribs variable in number up to thirty. Growth stages are sometimes prominent. Ears with three to five small riblets. Lower margin of the byssal notch with minute teeth. Margin usually crenulate. Found commonly from the low tide mark to a depth of 328 ft (100 m) on sand and gravel bottoms. Ranges from Iceland and Norway to Spain.

Kitten Scallop
1 in (2.5 cm)

Iceland Scallop, *Chlamys islandica* (Müller, 1776). Solid, both valves about the same convexity, oval-oblong, one ear twice as long as the other. With about fifty coarse, irregular ribs which split in two near the margin of the valve. Rarely, the ribs are grouped in twos, threes or fours. Colour usually dirty-grey or cream, but some may be tinged with peach, yellow or purplish both inside and out. A very common offshore species of Arctic Seas from Japan to Alaska to Puget Sound; Greenland to Massachusetts; and Iceland and Norway to the Shetland Islands.

Iceland Scallop
3 in (7.5 cm)

Variable Scallop, *Chlamys varia* (Linnaeus, 1758). Fan-shaped; anterior ears long. Colours variable. Sculpture of twenty-five to thirty-five prominent, spined ribs. Margins strongly crenulate. A common shallow-water species found under stones. Ranges from Denmark and the British Isles to the Mediterranean.

Variable Scallop
2.5 in (6.5 cm)

Sulcate Scallop, *Chlamys sulcata* (Müller, 1776). Shell small, solid, brittle; anterior ears about three times as long as the posterior ones. Colour dirty-white, yellowish or red-brown. Sculpture of twenty to forty radiating ribs with narrower riblets in between, usually clumped in threes or fours to give a sulcate surface. Ears with small riblets and with strong folds between the prominent byssal notch and the beaks. An uncommon, small scallop off the coasts of Scotland, Iceland, Norway and south to northwest Africa.

Sulcate Scallop
1.7 in (4 cm)

Pacific Spear Scallop, *Chlamys hastata hastata* (Sowerby, 1843). Shell solid, somewhat fan-shaped. Right valve (with byssal notch) with about eighteen to twenty primary, strongly spined ribs which have five to seven much smaller, weakly spined, secondary riblets in between; left valve with ten or eleven distantly spaced, scaled primary ribs, with twelve to sixteen weak, beaded secondary ribs in between. Colours are bright-orange, red or lemon. A southern form found offshore along the Californian coast. The subspecies *hericia* (Gould, 1850) or Pacific Pink Scallop has stronger ribs, is more spinose, and occurs from Alaska to Oregon.

Pacific Spear Scallop
2 in (5 cm)

Hinds' Scallop, *Chlamys rubida* (Hinds, 1845). With microscopic reticulations between the ribs near either the beaks or the margins of the valves. Left valve with three rows of spines on the primary ribs. Right valve, lighter in colour and with smoothish ribs. Common just offshore from Alaska, south to California.

Hinds' Scallop
2.5 in (6.5 cm)

Atlantic Bay Scallop, *Argopecten irradians* (Lamarck, 1819). Shell solid, almost circular, moderately inflated, with almost equal-sized ears. Each valve is about the same fatness, and the lower one is slightly lighter in colour. With seventeen or eighteen low, roundish ribs. Colour usually drab grey-brown with indistinct, dark-brown mottlings. Rarely yellowish or greyish orange. This is a common, edible scallop found among eelgrass beds in semi-enclosed bays in 3 to 65 ft (1–20 m). Ranges from the north shore of Cape Cod to New Jersey.

Atlantic Bay Scallop
2.5 in (6.5 cm)

Giant Rock Scallop, *Hinnites giganteus* (Gray, 1825). A heavy, massive shell, characterized by the early "*Chlamys*-like" shell at the beaks. Half-inch (1.5 cm) long young shells have a mauve spot on the inside of the hinge line. Adults are large, heavy with coarse, irregular radial riblets. Interior white with a purple hinge area. Attaches to rocks by the right valve. Moderately common offshore from 3 to 196 ft (1–60 m) from British Columbia to southern California.

Giant Rock Scallop
7 in (17.5 cm)

Hunchback Scallop, *Hinnites distortus* (da Costa, 1778). A small, permanently attached scallop, growing in its early life in the shape of a *Chlamys*, but then becoming irregularly shaped as it ages. Upper valve with about sixty prickly ribs. Colour white, yellow, reddish or brownish and often mottled. Lives in rock crevices or in kelp holdfasts. Ranges from Norway to the Azores.

Hunchback Scallop
1.5 in (3.5 cm)

Jingle Shells
(*Family Anomiidae*)

The thin, semi-translucent jingle shells have a remarkably strong shell and are frequently cast up on beaches. The lower valve has a round notch through which passes the strong attachment byssus. The top (or left) valve is usually convex. The flesh of the mollusc, although edible, has a very strong taste of alum. There are less than a dozen species in the family, and many have been spread by boats and floating logs.

Common Jingle Shell, *Anomia simplex* Orbigny, 1842. Shell strong, irregularly oval, smoothish and thin-shelled. Upper, free valve quite convex; lower valve flat with a large hole near the apex. Colour either translucent yellow or orange with a silvery sheen. Specimens buried in mud become blackened. Byssus forms a round, calcified base where it is attached. Common on logs and dead shells from Cape Cod to Texas and to Brazil.

Common Jingle Shell
1.5 in (4 cm)

False Pacific Jingle, *Pododesmus macroschisma* (Deshayes, 1839). Shell resembling a jingle shell, with very coarse, irregular radiating ribs. Upper valve with only two muscle scars. Lower valve with a hole. Colour greenish white and somewhat pearly. Common on stones, wharf pilings and other shells from 3 to 229 ft (1–70 m). Ranges from Japan to Alaska to Mexico.

False Pacific Jingle
3 in (7.5 cm)

File Clams
(*Family Limidae*)

These remarkable clams have many long tentacles extending from the margin of the mantle. They also produce a small byssal anchor and sometimes will build a protective nest of byssal threads. Many colourful species are tropical and hide under corals, while others are deep-sea and grow to over 5 inches (13 cm) in length.

Inflated File Clam, *Limaria inflata* (Gmelin, 1791). Shell thin but strong, white, obliquely elongate. One ear is twice as long as the other. The black resilium is small, triangular and located in the centre of the hinge. Valves rather well inflated. Sculpture of about twenty-five small, thread-like riblets which bear small beads where concentric growth lines cross. The margin of the valve bears a small prickle wherever a rib ends. A Mediterranean species extending north to France.

Inflated File Clam
1.5 in (4 cm)

Hians File Clam, *Limaria hians* (Gmelin, 1791). Shell thin, but strong, brown and very obliquely elongate. Byssal notch in the right anterior ear is very small. Wide dorsal gape. Beaks far apart, with fifty radiating riblets crossed by concentric lines. Tentacles red and orange. Common from Norway to the Azores.

Hians File Clam
1.5 in (4 cm)

Loscomb's File Clam, *Limaria loscombi* (Sowerby, 1820). Has a broad black cardinal area. Ears equal. Fifty distinct, beaded riblets. Margin with minute prickles. Offshore from Norway to the Mediterranean and Azores.

Loscomb's File Clam
0.8 in (2 cm)

Oysters
(*Family Ostreidae*)

The abundant and well-known oysters have served mankind as a seafood for many centuries. Of the three common species now living in western Europe, only one is native, the other two were probably introduced many years ago.

Giant Pacific Oyster, *Crassostrea gigas* (Thunberg, 1793). Shell large, of various shapes, but generally characterized by its elongate shape, its coarse, widely spaced, concentric lamellae or very coarse longitudinal fluting or ridges. Interior enamel-white, often with a faint purplish stain on the muscle scar. A common, shallow-water species of Japan now established from British Columbia to California. In Europe, where it was introduced many years ago it is called the **Portuguese Oyster**, *Crassostrea angulata* (Lamarck, 1818).

Giant Pacific Oyster
8 in (20 cm)

Eastern American Oyster, *Crassostrea virginica* (Gmelin, 1791). The valve margins are only slightly wavy or are straight. Lower valve cupped. The muscle scar is usually coloured a deep purple. Harvested commercially along the east coast of North America.

Eastern American Oyster
5 in (12.5 cm)

Common European Oyster, *Ostrea edulis* Linnaeus, 1758. Shell roughly circular in outline. Exterior rough, with deep radiating ribs and concentric ridges. Upper or right valve flat and brownish. Interior whitish with green or red-brown blotches. Common offshore from Norway to the Black Sea

Common European Oyster
4 in (10 cm)

Lucine Clams
(*Family Lucinidae*)

These circular, laterally compressed clams are recognized by the very long, narrow anterior muscle scar. The clams have very short siphons and hence there is no pallial sinus. The long foot is used to create a tunnel in the sandy mud for drawing in water to the gills.

Northeast Lucina, *Lucinoma filosa* (Stimpson, 1851). Almost circular, compressed, white, with a thin yellowish periostracum. Beaks small, close together and centrally located. No anterior lateral teeth present. Sculpture of sharp,

Northeast Lucina
2.5 in (6.5 cm)

concentric ridges. Common offshore from Newfoundland to north Florida and to Texas.

Western Ringed Lucina, *Lucinoma annulata* (Reeve, 1850). Oval to circular and slightly inflated, with strong raised, concentric threads. Colour chalky-grey to white, overlaid by a thin, greenish brown periostracum. Fairly common from 52 to 492 ft (16–150 m) from Alaska to southern California.

Western Ringed Lucina
2 in (5 cm)

Boreal Lucina, *Lucinoma borealis* (Linnaeus, 1758). Almost circular, solid, white with a thin brown periostracum. Strong concentric ridges are sometimes eroded away. Two small cardinal teeth in each valve. One of them is bifid. Margin of valves smooth. Lives in shallow water to 328 ft (100 m) in sandy mud. Ranges from Norway to the Baltic and south to the Mediterranean.

Boreal Lucina
1.2 in (3 cm)

Cardita and Astarte Clams
(*Families Carditidae and Astartidae*)

These families of small, solid clams serve as a major source of food for Arctic bottom-feeding fish. The clams are usually ovate, with the beaks near the centre, and with a thick, dark-brown periostracum. There is no pallial sinus scar.

Fine-ribbed Cardita, *Cyclocardia borealis* (Conrad, 1831). Shell strong and obliquely heart-shaped. Beaks elevated and turned forward. Has about twenty rounded, moderately rough or beaded radial ribs. Colour white, but usually covered with a thick, velvety brownish periostracum. Lunule small but very deeply sunk. A common offshore species ranging from Labrador to off North Carolina.

Fine-ribbed Cardita
1 in (2.5 cm)

Smooth Astarte, *Astarte castanea* (Say, 1822). Shell solid, fairly small, trigonal in outline and quite compressed. Beaks pointed and hooked forward. Lunule large and shallow. Exterior smoothish. Colour a glossy light-brown. Inner margins finely crenulate. This is a common offshore species ranging from Nova Scotia to off New Jersey.

Smooth Astarte
1 in (2.5 cm)

Sulcate Astarte, *Astarte sulcata* (da Costa, 1778). Shell oval, slightly compressed, with twenty-four to fifty-five prominent, broad radial ribs. Lunule and escutcheon prominent. Inner margin finely crenulate. Periostracum light-brown. Colour of shell white to salmon-pink. Common offshore from Greenland and Iceland to the Mediterranean.

Sulcate Astarte
1 in (2.5 cm)

Cockles
(*Family Cardiidae*)

The well-known cockle family is worldwide in distribution and contains several dozen genera and several hundred living species. The shells vary from the large and copious *Cardium* of West Africa to the flat, heart-shaped *Corculum* of the East Indies. The foot of the cockles is large and muscular and the siphons are quite short. The ligament is external.

European Spiny Cockle, *Acanthocardia aculeata* (Linnaeus, 1767). Thin-shelled but strong, broadly oval in outline and with twenty to twenty-two strong, radial ribs, each bearing a row of spines down the middle. Right valve with two anterior laterals and one posterior lateral. Interior of valves radially furrowed. Colour yellowish brown, with darker blotches. Subtidal to 98 ft (30 m). Rare in Britain; commoner southward into the Mediterranean.

European Spiny Cockle
3 in (7.5 cm)

Sand Cockle, *Acanthocardia spinosa* (Lightfoot, 1786). Broadly oval, with about thirty-five small, squarish radial ribs, those at the anterior end bearing smooth, rounded scales, and those at the posterior end having numerous, short spines. Colour yellow-brown. A Mediterranean species ranging north to Portugal.

Sand Cockle
2.5 in (6.5 cm)

Tuberculate Cockle, *Acanthocardia tuberculata* (Linnaeus, 1758). Elongate-oval, with the beaks near the anterior end. Twenty-one to twenty-three weakly beaded radial ribs. Colour light brown. A common shallow-water cockle from the British Isles to the Mediterranean.

Morton's Egg Cockle, *Laevicardium mortoni* (Conrad, 1830). Thin-shelled, small, swollen and oval. Surface smooth, glossy, yellowish brown with darker zigzag markings and with fine concentric ridges which may be minutely pimpled. This common food for ducks lives in sand from 3 to 19 ft (1–6 m) of water. It ranges from Cape Cod to Texas.

Heavy Egg Cockle, *Laevicardium crassum* (Gmelin, 1791). Shell solid, obliquely oval, with the beaks well in front of the midline. Colour dirty yellow, sometimes with red and brown blotches and zigzag markings, especially near the beaks. Periostracum thin, greenish yellow. Sculpture of forty to fifty very faint, smooth radial riblets. No spines or scales. Interior cream-tan. Margins crenulate. This common species lives among broken shell and gravel from Norway to the Mediterranean and the Cape Verde Islands.

Greenland Cockle, *Serripes groenlandicus* (Bruguière, 1789). Shell fairly large, solid, inflated, and with a slight gape at the pointed posterior end. Exterior smoothish, brownish grey. Interior dull-white. Beaks inflated. Ligament large and strong. No

Tuberculate Cockle
2.5 in (6.5 cm)

Morton's Egg Cockle
1 in (2.5 cm)

Heavy Egg Cockle
3 in (7.5 cm)

lunule or pallial sinus. Foot of animal mottled red. Common offshore from 19 to 393 ft (6–120 m) in Arctic Seas to Massachusetts and to Puget Sound, Washington State.

Greenland Cockle
4 in (10 cm)

Nuttall's Cockle, *Clinocardium nuttallii* (Conrad, 1837). Shell fairly large, roundly oval, moderately compressed and usually with thirty-three to thirty-seven coarse, radial ribs with half-moon beads. Older specimens are worn smooth. Beaks nearer the anterior end and considerably rolled in. Interior whitish, with the margins showing distinct ribbing. Colour drab-grey, with a thin, brownish yellow periostracum. A common offshore sand-loving cockle ranging from the Bering Sea and Alaska to off southern California.

Nuttall's Cockle
4 in (10 cm)

Iceland Cockle, *Clinocardium ciliatum* (Fabricius, 1780). Fairly large, roundly oval, moderately compressed, with thirty-two to thirty-eight ridged radial ribs which are crossed by coarse, concentric lines of growth. Exterior drab-greyish yellow with weak, narrow, concentric bands of darker colour. Interior ivory. Periostracum grey. Common from Alaska to Puget Sound, and from Greenland to Massachusetts.

Iceland Cockle
3 in (7.5 cm)

Common European Cockle, *Cerastoderma edule* (Linnaeus, 1758). Shell solid, broadly oval, with inrolled beaks almost touching each other. With twenty-two to twenty-eight squarish radial ribs, each with numerous weak scales. Right valve with two anterior and two posterior lateral teeth. Interior of valves white and stained brown around the muscle scars. Margins crenulate inside. Abundant near estuaries from Norway to Portugal and West Africa.

Common European Cockle
5 in (12.5 cm)

✦

Trough Clams
(*Family Mactridae*)

Called trough shells in England and surf clams in New England, these large, smooth clams are recognized by the small, spoon-shaped compartment, or chondrophore, in the centre of the hinge. Into this fits the pad-like, black resilium which keeps the valves ajar.

Californian Mactra
2 in (5 cm)

California Mactra, *Mactra californica* Conrad, 1837. Shell elongate-oval, moderately fragile, smooth, and with peculiar, concentric undulations on the beaks. The velvety yellowish brown periostracum forms an angular ridge along the top posterior edge of each valve. This small species is fairly common in lagoons of California, but rarer in Puget Sound.

Hooked Surf Clam
2.5 in (6.5 cm)

Hooked Surf Clam, *Spisula falcata* (Gould, 1850). Elongate at the narrower anterior end. Low beaks nearer the rounded posterior end. Anterior upper margin slightly concave. Exterior chalky, with a brown, shiny periostracum. Common from Washington to California.

Stimpson's Surf Clam, *Spisula polynyma* (Stimpson, 1860). Large, solid. Colour dirty-white with a coarse, varnish-like periostracum. Pallial sinus large. Common offshore from the Arctic Seas to Rhode Island; Japan to Puget Sound.

Stimpson's Surf Clam
4 in (10 cm)

Atlantic Surf Clam, *Spisula solidissima* (Dillwyn, 1817). Shell large, strong, elongate-oval and smoothish, except for small, irregular growth lines. Lateral teeth bear very tiny, sawtooth ridges. Colour yellowish white with a thin, yellowish brown periostracum. In the hinge, the small oval, black-brown ligament which is close to the dorsal margin does not have a shelly ridge between it and the larger chondrophore cup, as is the case in *Mactra*. An abundant shallow-water, edible species commercially dredged offshore. Occurs from Nova Scotia to off South Carolina.

Atlantic Surf Clam
5 in (12.5 cm)

Alaskan Gaper, *Tresus capax* (Gould, 1850). Shell large, oval-elongate, with a dip or bulge in the ventral margin. Gapes at the posterior end. Cardinal teeth small, and lateral very small. Ligament external and separated from the cartilage pit by a shelly plate. Common in shallow water in sandy mud from Alaska to northern California.

Alaskan Gaper
8 in (20 cm)

Rayed Trough Clam, *Mactra corallina* (Linnaeus, 1758). Shell brittle, ovate; beaks in the midline and curled inward and slightly forward. Colour creamy white with purplish around the beaks, and usually with brown rays. Periostracum light-brown. Interior purplish white. Pallial sinus deep. Widely distributed from Norway to the Black Sea and to Senegal.

Rayed Trough Clam
1.5 in (4 cm)

Solid Trough Clam, *Spisula solida* (Linnaeus, 1758). Shell of medium size, solid, ovate, beaks central and the exterior smoothish, except for irregular growth stoppages. Shell whitish grey; periostracum light-brown but usually worn away. Pallial sinus short and rounded at the end. Adductor muscle scars recessed. Hinge teeth strong; with a fairly large chondrophore. Shape of this clam may vary from truncate to oval. Found from 3 to 492 ft (1–150 m) from Finland to Spain and Morocco.

Solid Trough Clam
5 in (12.5 cm)

Subtruncate Trough Clam, *Spisula subtruncata* (da Costa, 1778). Fairly small, ovate-triangular and solid; beaks nearer the front end. Colour greyish white to brownish. External ligament is short and narrow just behind the beaks. Sculpture of coarse, concentric lines. Lunule and escutcheon with fine ridges. Laterals finely serrated. Pallial sinus shallow. An abundant offshore sand-lover occurring from Norway to the Black Sea and the Canary Islands.

Subtruncate Trough Clam
1 in (2.5 cm)

Flat Furrow Clam, *Scrobicularia plana* (da Costa, 1778). Shell almost round in outline; compressed; with the beaks almost at the centre. Colour greyish brown or light-yellow. Periostracum brown, velvety, but usually worn away. Internal ligament large, obliquely slanting and set in the chondrophore. This intertidal clam is in the family Scrobiculariidae. It lives from Norway south to Senegal.

Flat Furrow Clam
2.5 in (6.5 cm)

European Otter Clam, *Lutraria lutraria* (Linnaeus, 1758). Shell fairly large, solid, oval-elongate in outline and gaping at both ends; beaks nearer the front end and directed inward. Colour yellowish brown with an olive-brown, thin periostracum. Internal ligament black, triangular and set in a large chondrophore. Pallial sinus large and oval at the closed end. Lower margin of the pallial sinus scar is separated from the pallial line below it. Common from 3 to 295 ft (1–90 m) from Norway to the Baltic, Mediterranean and West Africa.

European Otter Clam
5 in (12.5 cm)

Oblong Otter Clam, *Lutraria magna* (da Costa, 1778). Shell similar to the European Otter Clam, but more elongate, with the dorsal margin behind the beak concave, and with the beaks closer to the front end. The lower section of the pallial sinus is confluent with the main pallial scar. This member of the subfamily Lutrariinae is a common, shallow-water clam living from the British Isles to the Mediterranean.

Oblong Otter Clam
6 in (15 cm)

Arctic Wedge Clam, *Mesodesma arctatum* (Conrad, 1830). Heavy for its size, elongate-oval, with the posterior end truncate and having a very short pallial sinus. Anterior end narrower and compressed. Chondrophore oblique. The lateral teeth have fine, comb-like teeth on each side. Belongs to the family Mesodesmatidae. Common offshore from Greenland and Labrador to Maryland.

Arctic Wedge Clam
1.5 in (4 cm)

Razor Clams
(*Family Pharellidae*)

This widespread family of razorfish or razor clams is predominantly a cold-water group characterized by their elongate and compressed shape, reduced hinge teeth and glossy, smooth periostracum.

Pacific Razor Clam, *Siliqua patula* (Dixon, 1788). Shell lightweight but strong, oval-oblong, laterally compressed. Periostracum varnish-like and olive-green in colour. Interior glossy and whitish with a purple flush. Internal rib below the tiny cardinals descend, obliquely towards the anterior ventral margin. An abundant, edible species found in shallow water from Alaska to central California.

Pacific Razor Clam
5 in (12.5 cm)

Squamate Razor Clam, *Siliqua squamata* Blainville, 1827. With a prominent internal rib descending straight down towards the ventral margin. Dull-white with a glossy periostracum with chestnut-brown, concentric bands. Uncommon offshore from Newfoundland to Cape Cod.

Squamate Razor Clam
3 in (7.5 cm)

Atlantic Razor Clam, *Siliqua costata* Say, 1822. Shell delicate, compressed, thin-shelled. Exterior with a shiny, greenish periostracum. Interior glossy, purplish white, with a strong white rib. Very common in shallow water in firm sand from the Gulf of St. Lawrence to off North Carolina.

Atlantic Razor Clam
2 in (5 cm)

Atlantic Jackknife Clam, *Ensis directus* (Conrad, 1843). Shell long, cylindrical, smooth, moderately curved and with sharp edges. Gapes widely at each end. Shell white, covered with a thin, varnish-like, brownish green periostracum. Left valve has two very small, vertical cardinals near the beak end, and each valve has a long, low, inconspicuous posterior lateral tooth. A common, edible species living in sand burrows from southern Labrador to South Carolina, but commonest in New England.

Atlantic Jackknife Clam
9 in (22.5 cm)

Narrow Jackknife Clam, *Ensis ensis* (Linnaeus, 1758). Slightly bowed. Colour tan-white with reddish brown blotches. Anterior end rounded. Periostracum greenish brown to yellowish green and glossy. Right valve with one cardinal and two lateral teeth; left valve with two cardinals and two

Narrow Jackknife Clam
4 in (10 cm)

laterals. Fairly common in silty sand from the intertidal zone down to 65 ft (20 m). Ranges from Norway to the Mediterranean.

Giant Razor Clam, *Ensis siliqua* (Linnaeus, 1758). Elongate-rectangular with rounded, gaping ends and almost straight margins. Beaks inconspicuous at the anterior end. Colour white with reddish streaks and blotches. Periostracum dark-green. Interior white with purplish tints. This common species is larger and stouter than the Narrow Jackknife Clam. Occurs from Norway to the Baltic and into the Mediterranean.

Giant Razor Clam
8 in (20 cm)

Blunt Jackknife Clam, *Solen sicarius* Gould, 1850. Shell elongate-rectangular, with very slightly curved dorsal and ventral margins. The anterior beak end is obliquely truncate, and the posterior end is rounded and slightly compressed. *Solen* differs from *Ensis* in having only a single tooth usually located at the very anterior end of the valve. Periostracum varnish-like and olive greenish. Common on sandy mud flats from British Columbia to California.

Blunt Jackknife Clam
3.5 in (9 cm)

European Razor Clam, *Solen vagina* Linnaeus, 1758. With parallel margins; obliquely truncate at the anterior end and squarely rounded at the other end. Colour yellowish with brownish growth lines. Each valve has one cardinal but no laterals. Synonym is *S. marginatus* Montagu (and Pulteney). This species is found just offshore where it burrows into

European Razor Clam
5 in (12.5 cm)

sandy bottoms. Ranges from Norway into the Baltic and down into the Mediterranean.

Bean Razor Clam, *Pharus legumen* (Linnaeus, 1758). Shell elongate-cylindrical, brittle, with the inconspicuous beaks almost centrally located. Both ends gaping and rounded. Colour yellowish white with a yellowish green periostracum. Ligament prominent, external and dark-brown. Right valve with a tiny vertical cardinal and one long, ridge-like anterior lateral and a short, projecting posterior lateral. White rib inside. Pallial sinus short. Common from Norway to the Mediterranean.

Bean Razor Clam
5 in (12.5 cm)

Tellins
(*Family Tellinidae*)

This worldwide family of bivalves is known for its very colourful shells with a simple architecture. Most are smooth, laterally compressed and rather thin-shelled. There is a slight twist at the posterior end. There are two small cardinal teeth, one of which is bifid.

Great Alaskan Tellin
3.5 in (9 cm)

Great Alaskan Tellin, *Tellina lutea* Wood, 1828. Shell strong, elongate-oval, quite compressed laterally and with a posterior twist to the right. Chalky white, commonly with a pink flush.

Periostracum greenish brown. External ligament prominent. Pallial sinus three-quarters the length of the interior. Commonly found from 3 to 118 ft (1–36 m) from Japan to Alaska and northern British Columbia.

Bodegas Tellin, *Tellina bodegensis* Hinds, 1845. Narrowly elongate, laterally compressed, with the posterior end narrow and drawn out. Dorsal and ventral margins almost parallel. Pallial line long and narrow. Exterior with concentric threads. Fairly common from 3 to 98 ft (1–30 m) in sand from Canada to Mexico.

Bodegas Tellin
2 in (5 cm)

Salmon Tellin, *Tellina nuculoides* (Reeve, 1845). Small, oval, white with widely spaced growth lines. Interior with a rose tint. Common from the Aleutians to central California.

Salmon Tellin
0.5 in (1.2 cm)

Story Tellin, *Tellina fabula* (Gmelin, 1791). Shell small, elongate-oval, with the posterior end pointed. Right valve slightly more convex than the left. Posterior end twisted towards the right. Colour white or tinged with yellow or orange. Periostracum yellowish. Sculpture of concentric lines. In the left valve diagonal lines cross them. Pallial sinus deep, broad, quadrate. Common in sand 3 to 164 ft (1–50 m). Occurs from Norway to the Black Sea and north west Africa.

Story Tellin
0.7 in (2 cm)

Donax Tellin, *Tellina donacina* Linnaeus, 1758. Shell small, thin-shelled but strong; right valve slightly more convex than the left one. External ligament large. Colour grey to yellowish with pink rays; sometimes all-white. Sculpture of many evenly spaced, concentric ridges. Interior pearly white with yellow or pink blush. Pallial sinus scar almost touches the anterior adductor muscle. A common, shallow-water species in coarse sand from the Orkney south to the Black Sea and Azores.

Donax Tellin
1 in (2.5 cm)

Thick Tellin, *Arcopagia crassa* (Pennant, 1777). Circular in outline; beaks almost in the centre; somewhat compressed. Colour dirty tan with the beaks tinged with orange or pink radial rays. Periostracum yellow-brown. Exterior with concentric ridges with fine radiating lines showing between. Common offshore from Norway to Senegal.

Thick Tellin
2.5 in (6.5 cm)

Chalky Macoma, *Macoma calcarea* (Gmelin, 1791). Oval-elongate, moderately compressed, but somewhat inflated at the larger anterior end. Beaks three-fifths the way towards the narrow, slightly twisted posterior end. *Macoma* do not have lateral teeth. Grey periostracum usually worn away except at margins. Pallial sinus in left valve does not reach the anterior muscle scar. Much shorter in right valve. A common cold-water species found offshore in Arctic waters from Greenland to New York, and from the Bering Sea to Washington State.

Chalky Macoma
2 in (5 cm)

Balthica Macoma, *Macoma balthica* (Linnaeus, 1758). Shell fairly small, oval, moderately compressed. Colour dull whitish, sometimes flushed with pink. Periostracum thin, grey and flakes off when dry. Pallial sinus reaches halfway to anterior muscle scar in left valve. An abundant intertidal and offshore species in Arctic waters south to estuaries in Norway to Portugal; Greenland to off Georgia.

Balthica Macoma
1 in (2.5 cm

Doleful Macoma, *Macoma moesta* (Deshayes, 1855). Shell ovate, inflated, with the beaks two-thirds the way back from the larger, rounded end. Periostracum yellowish olive. Posterior end short, slightly angular, and finely wrinkled at the angle. Pallial sinus rounded, smaller in right valve. Common offshore in muddy areas. Arctic Seas; Greenland and Alaska.

Doleful Macoma
1.5 in (4 cm)

Tenta Macoma, *Macoma tenta* (Say, 1837). Shell oval-elongate, somewhat compressed, rather fragile. Colour white with a delicate iridescence on the smooth exterior. Posterior end slightly twisted to the left. Interior glossy white, tinted with yellow and with fine radiating lines, which produce a finely serrated margin. Two diverging cardinals in the right valve, a single one in the left. A common shallow-water species from Cape Cod to Florida and to Brazil.

Tenta Macoma
0.8 in (2 cm)

Bent-nose Macoma, *Macoma nasuta* (Conrad, 1837). Rather compressed and strongly twisted to the right at the posterior end. Pallial sinus scar in the left valve reaches the anterior muscle scar. External ligament large and black. A very common Pacific coast

Bent-nose Macoma
3 in (7.5 cm)

species living in mud in quiet waters from shore to 164 feet (50 m); southern Alaska to Mexico.

Fouled Macoma, *Macoma inquinata* (Deshayes, 1855). Shell oval-elongate, moderately inflated, very slightly twisted at the posterior end. Pallial sinus in left valve almost reaches the bottom of the anterior muscle scar. Colour chalky white. Periostracum grey and with fine concentric growth lines. Posterior ventral margin with a weak embayment. A moderately common, offshore clam ranging from Japan and the Bering Sea to off southern California.

Fouled Macoma
2 in (5 cm)

✦

Sunset Clams
(*Family Psammobiidae*)

These fairly large clams resemble the tellin clams but are generally larger, with purple and reddish colours, and with a large, external ligament that is attached to a prominent, shelly ridge. No lateral teeth. Pallial sinus is large.

Californian Sunset Clam, *Gari californica* (Conrad, 1849). Elongate-oval, fairly strong; the low beaks are nearer the anterior end. Sculpture of strong, irregular, concentric growth lines. Colour dirty white or cream, and may have faint, narrow, radial rays of purple. Periostracum brownish

California Sunset Clam
4 in (10 cm)

grey. Common from 3 to 164 ft (1–50 m), and often washed ashore after storms. Ranges from the Aleutians to southern California.

Depressed Sunset Clam, *Gari depressa* (Pennant, 1777). Shell solid, evenly elongate, with the beaks almost at the centre. Right valve a little more convex. Colour cream with purplish rays. Periostracum thick and greenish brown. Lives in coarse sand in 3 to 164 ft (1–50 m). Ranges from the North Sea to West Africa.

Depressed Sunset Clam
2.5 in (6.5 cm)

Faroes Sunset Clam, *Gari fervensis* (Gmelin, 1791). Elongate, with the posterior and narrower end bearing a rounded keel. Surface with crowded, concentric threads. Colour of variable purples and brownish pinks with a few rays. A common offshore species from Norway to West Africa.

Faroes Sunset Clam
2 in (5 cm)

Tellin-like Sunset Clam, *Gari tellinella* (Lamarck, 1818). Shell small, solid, oval-elongate in outline. Colour whitish cream with tints of orange, red or purplish. Periostracum very thin. Ligament brown with red bands. Sculpture of fine concentric and radiating lines. Growth stoppages evident. Right valve with two bifid cardinals. No lateral teeth. A common, shallow-water clam found from Iceland and Norway to the Mediterranean.

Tellin-like Sunset Clam
1 in (2.5 cm)

Rose Petal Semele, *Semele rubropicta* Dall, 1871. In the family Semelidae, the black resilium is in an oblique gutter which is buried in the hinge. Shell oval-elongate, with the beaks nearer the front end. Has irregular growth lines and many radial incised lines. Colour chalky grey to tan with faint rays of light-mauve. Interior glossy-white, with mauve at both ends of the hinge. Uncommon offshore. Ranges from Alaska to Mexico.

Rose Petal Semele
1.5 in (4 cm)

White Abra Clam, *Abra alba* (Wood, 1815). Shell small, white, brittle, broadly oval; posterior with a slight twist to the right. Hinge weak and narrow, with the narrow, brown internal ligament in a grooved, triangular chondrophore. Pallial sinus large. Common in mud or muddy gravel from low tide mark to 216 feet (66 m). Ranges from Norway to the Black Sea and to Senegal.

White Abra Clam
0.8 in (2 cm)

✦

Oxheart Clams
(*Family Glossidae*)

Popular as a food and desired by shell collectors, the Oxheart Clam is the only member of this strange family of bivalves in the Northern Hemisphere. The beaks are strongly curled in, and there is no lunule nor any pallial sinus scar.

Oxheart Clam, *Glossus humanus* (Linnaeus, 1758). Shell medium-sized, solid, globular, without any gape, and with strongly enrolled, swollen beaks. Ligament brown and external. Sculpture of fine concentric and radial lines. Exterior tan, sometimes with reddish streaks. Periostracum greenish brown. A common offshore species ranging from Iceland and Norway to the Mediterranean.

Oxheart Clam
3 in (7.5 cm)

Ocean Quahog, *Arctica islandica* (Linnaeus, 1767). Oval in outline, moderately inflated. Colour yellowish to brown; periostracum thick, chestnut-brown. No pallial sinus. A common, edible offshore hardshell clam ranging from Iceland to France; Labrador to off North Carolina. In the family Arcticidae.

Ocean Quahog
4 in (10 cm)

Zebra Mussel, *Dreissena polymorpha* (Pallas, 1771). Shell shaped like a *Mytilus* mussel. Anterior muscle attached to a shelf-like platform in the apical region. Byssus strong. Colour tan with dark zebra stripes. Common in freshwater in Europe and now in the Great Lakes of United States.

Zebra Mussel
1 in (2.5 cm)

Venus Clams
(*Family Veneridae*)

This is a large and diverse family used extensively for food in many parts of the world. Many have colourful patterns and intricate sculpturing.

Warty Venus, *Venus verrucosa* Linnaeus, 1758. Circular in outline and rather swollen. Colour greyish white to brownish cream. Periostracum brown but usually worn away. Lunules broad, heart-shaped, brown, with fine radiating threads. Escutcheon prominent in the left valve. Pallial sinus small and triangular. A common, edible clam found in shallow water from the British Isles to the Mediterranean and Canary Islands.

Warty Venus
2.5 in (6 cm)

Chamber Venus, *Circomphalus casinus* (Linnaeus, 1758). Circular in outline and with numerous, smooth, raised concentric ridges. Colour whitish tan, sometimes with reddish brown rays. Inner margin of valves crenulate. Pallial sinus short and triangular. A common offshore species ranging from Norway to Senegal.

Chamber Venus
2 in (5 cm)

Northern Quahog or Hardshell Clam, *Mercenaria mercenaria* (Linnaeus, 1758). Ovate-trigonal, inflated. Exterior grey with fine growth threads. Centre of valves are smoothish. Interior white with purple stains. A common, edible clam found in shallow water from Quebec to Texas. Introduced to California and England.

Northern Quahog
4 in (10 cm)

Common Pacific Littleneck, *Protothaca staminea* (Conrad, 1837). Solid, subovate, laterally compressed, beaks nearer the anterior end. Sculpture of fine concentric and radial riblets which form beads at the anterior end of the shell. Radial riblets stronger on the middle of the valves. Lunule feeble; escutcheon absent. Colour rusty-brown with a purplish cast. This common, edible, shallow-water clam is quite variable in sculpturing and colouring. Ranges from the Aleutians to Mexico.

Common Pacific Littleneck
2 in (5 cm)

Filipino Venus or Japanese Littleneck, *Ruditapes philippinarum* (Adams and Reeve, 1850). Subovate, laterally compressed, with beaks nearer the anterior end. Lunule smooth and incised. Escutcheon smooth and bordered by a low ridge. With radial threads, those at posterior end beaded. Interior purplish. This eastern Asian species was introduced to Puget Sound and California.

Filipino Venus
2 in (5 cm)

Decussate Venus or Carpet-shell, *Venerupis decussata* (Linnaeus, 1758). Broadly oval, with numerous radial riblets crossed by fine concentric growth lines. Colours of greys, yellows and browns, sometimes with rays and streaks. Interior glossy white with an orange tinge, rarely purplish. Pallial sinus deep. Margin smooth. Common in shallow water from Norway to Mediterranean.

Decussate Venus
2 in (5 cm)

Morrhua Venus, *Pitar morrhuanus* Linsley, 1848. Shell small, obese, oval-elongate, with a large, elongate lunule. Beaks large and towards the anterior end. Anterior left lateral fits into a well-developed socket in the right valve. Middle left cardinal large; posterior right cardinal bifid. Exterior dull-grey to brownish red, with numerous heavy lines of growth. This is a fairly common offshore clam ranging from the

Morrhua Venus
1 in (2.5 cm)

Gulf of St. Lawrence to off North Carolina where it serves as an important food for bottom fish.

Smooth Washington Clam, *Saxidomus gigantea* (Deshayes, 1839). Solid, oblong, heavy, with fairly coarse, crowded concentric threads and fine growth stoppages. Valves gape slightly at the back end. Hinge with four or five cardinal teeth in the right valve, four in the left. Pallial sinus long and fairly narrow. No lunule. Ligament large. Colour greyish white. A common food clam in Alaska. Extends southward to northern California.

Smooth Washington Clam
3 in (7.5 cm)

Wolf Dosinia, *Dosinia lupinus* (Poli, 1791). Shell solid, circular in outline, moderately compressed. Beaks in front of the midline. Ligament deeply inset. Lunule short, heart-shaped and with fine radial ridges. Sculpture of fine concentric ridges crossed by faint radiating lines. Three cardinal teeth in each valve. Pallial sinus triangular, deep. Margin smooth. Lives in sand and silty mud from 3 to 426 ft (1–130 m) from Iceland and Norway to the Mediterranean and south to West Africa.

Wolf Dosinia
1.5 in (4 cm)

Mature Dosinia, *Dosinia exoleta* (Linnaeus, 1758). Shell circular and laterally compressed. Similar to the Wolf Dosinia, but the lunule is flatter, the valves are flatter, the pallial sinus is larger and broader and the exterior is not as glossy. The colour is light-brown, with numerous fine, radial, reddish brown streaks, usually accumulating at former growth

Mature Dosinia
2 in (5 cm)

stoppages. While buried in sand, it leaves two small round holes marking the presence of the two siphons. The clam occurs from the intertidal zone down to about 229 ft (70 m) of water. It has a wide range, from Norway to Portugal, into the Mediterranean, and south to Senegal and Gabon.

Kennerley's Venus, *Humilaria kennerleyi* (Reeve, 1863). Shell fairly large, elongate-oval, laterally compressed. Beaks near the smaller, anterior end. Exterior with sharp, neatly spaced, concentric ribs whose edges are bent upwards. Colour and texture resembles grey Portland cement. Margin of shell finely crenulate. A fairly common collector's item occurring offshore from 19 to 98 ft (6–30 m) from Alaska to northern California.

Kennerley's Venus
3.5 in (9 cm)

Hearty Ruppellaria, *Rupellaria carditoides* (Conrad, 1837). Oblong-ovate, obese, solid, pure-white. Variable in shape because it bores into hard rock. Exterior chalky greyish white with coarse, irregular, concentric growth lines. Radial sculpture of peculiar, fine, scratched lines crowded together. No lunule or escutcheon. Hinge without lateral teeth. Three cardinals in the left valve; two in right valve. Pallial sinus well-developed. Nepionic shell at beak is oblong. Common in rocks in shallow water from Vancouver Island to Baja California, Mexico.

Hearty Rupellaria
1.5 in (4 cm)

False Angel Wing, or American Piddock, *Petricola pholadiformis* (Lamarck, 1818). Shell elongate, rather fragile and chalky-white.

Numerous radial ribs; the anterior ten or so are larger and bear prominent scales. Ligament external and located just posterior to the beaks. Cardinal teeth quite long and pointed. A very common clay and peat-moss borer. Rarely in limestone in Europe. Frequents estuaries. Ranges from the Gulf of St. Lawrence to Texas and south to Uruguay; introduced to western Europe where it has spread from Norway to West Africa.

False Angel Wing
2 in (5 cm)

Arctic Saxicave, *Hiatella arctica* (Linnaeus, 1767). Shell chalky-white, oblong, usually somewhat misshapen because it bores into rocks and small boulders. No definite teeth in the thickened hinge of adults. Pallial line discontinuous. Periostracum grey and thin. Sometimes with a radial rib at the posterior end, which may bear scales. Common also in kelp holdfasts and rock crevices subtidally. Arctic Seas to California; Labrador to Uruguay; Norway to the Mediterranean and Azores.

Arctic Saxicave
2 in (5 cm)

Sand-gapers or Soft-shell Clams
(*Family Myidae*)

The gapers, or soft-shell clams, are popular seafood in the Northern Hemisphere, both in the New World and Old World.

The chalky, white shells are easily broken. The valves gape at the posterior end where a long, fused pair of siphons extend.

Sand-gaper, or Soft-shell Clam, *Mya arenaria* Linnaeus, 1758. Shell chalky, brittle, elliptical, oblong, and gaping at the posterior end. Colour white to greyish, with a thin grey to straw periostracum. Chondrophore in left valve is long, spoon-shaped and shallow. An abundant, intertidal, mud or sand flat species fished commercially in New England. It has a wide range from southern Labrador to off North Carolina; from northern Norway to France and from Alaska to northern California.

Sand-gaper
4 in (10 cm)

Blunt Gaper, or Truncate Soft-shell Clam, *Mya truncata* Linnaeus, 1758. Shell similar to the Sand-gaper, but smaller, abruptly truncate at the posterior siphonal end, and the lower margin of the pallial line is confluent with the pallial sinus scar. A common Arctic species found offshore south to Massachusetts, Portugal, Washington State and Japan.

Blunt Gaper
2.5 in (6.5 cm)

Common Basket-shell, or Fat Corbula, *Corbula gibba* (Olivi, 1792). Shell small, solid, with the right valve deeper and larger than the left one which fits into it. Left valve with chondrophore and a deep triangular pit. Pallial sinus absent. Colour cream, with a brownish periostracum. In family Corbulidae.

Common Basket-shell
0.5 in (1.2 cm)

Geoduck (goo-ee-duck), *Panopea abrupta* (Conrad, 1849). Shell large, inflated, elongate, thick-shelled and gaping at both ends. Coarse, concentric, wavy lines especially noticeable near the small, central, depressed beaks. Periostracum thin and yellowish. Exterior dirty-white to cream; interior semi-glossy white. Hinge with a single, large, horizontal thickening. Common in mud 2 or 3 ft (60–90 cm). Ranges from Alaska to the Gulf of California, but commercially fished in Washington and Oregon.

Geoduck
9 in (22.5 cm)

European Piddock, *Pholas dactylus* Linnaeus, 1758. Shell brittle, elongate, gaping at both ends; umbones near the anterior end and covered with two elongate, separate, calcareous protoplax plates. On the back edge is the small, central mesoplax, and posterior to that is the long, narrow, calcareous, metaplax plate. Within the valve and under the umbonal reflection is the long, narrow, projecting apophysis. Anterior end of valve with about forty spined, radiating ribs. Remainder of valve with concentric ridges. Pallial sinus scar wide and shallow. Bores into many subtidal substrates, including sand, peat, wood, shale and sandstone. Ranges from Norway to the Black Sea and from Labrador to Delaware.

European Piddock
5 in (12.5 cm)

Paper Piddock, *Pholadidea loscombiana* Turton, 1819. Shell fragile, elongate-oval, divided into two regions by the umbonal-ventral sulcus. Gaping anterior end may be sealed over by a smooth, bulbous callum. Tooth-like apophyses are small, fragile and project from beneath the umbones. Edge of wide gape is serrated. Pallial sinus broad and deep. Common in clay, peat and sandstone in British Isles and coast of France.

Paper Piddock
1 in (2.5 cm)

Striate Nartesia, *Martesia striata* (Linnaeus, 1758). Variable in shape, usually pear-shaped, producing a round, smooth callum over the wide foot-gape in the adult. Posterior end compressed and rounded in outline. Anterior to the oblique external furrow are numerous, finely denticulate riblets. White in colour, with a tan periostracum. Sculpture of fine concentric parallel threads. Apophyses long, thin. Pallial sinus deep. Common in floating or submerged wood from North Carolina south to Brazil. Introduced to the British Isles.

Striate Martesia
1 in (2.5 cm)

Gabb's Piddock, *Penitella gabbi* (Tryon, 1863). Shell thin but strong, elongate-oval, with an oblique, external sulcus, in front of which is the wide, oblique gape for the foot. Anterior end with numerous radial, beaded ribs. Mesoplax plate in the adult has broad, lateral wings. Siphonoplax absent. Moderately common in clay and sandstone. Ranges from Drier Bay, Alaska, to San Pedro, California.

Gabb's Piddock
2 in (5 cm)

Gould's Shipworm, *Bankia gouldi* Bartsch, 1908. There are many species of *Teredo* and *Bankia* shipworms throughout the Northern Hemisphere, and a scientific monograph must be consulted in order properly to identify them. The drilling is done by a pair of cup-like shelly valves. The soft parts of the bivalve are encased in long, shelly, white tunnels. The exit to the water is protected by a pair of "feathery" pallets. The latter are used in identifying species. Great destruction to wooden ships and wharf pilings done by shipworms and by the crustacean, *Limnoria*.

Gould's Shipworm Tubes
8 in (20 cm)

Acknowledgments

The author wishes to thank the curators and staff of the Departments of Mollusks at the Museum of Comparative Zoology, Harvard University; the Academy of Natural Sciences of Philadelphia and the U.S. National Museum in Washington D.C., for their kindness in permitting him to study and photograph the molluscs under their care.

The publisher wishes to thank the following photographers for their illustrations which appear on pages 15 and 119: David Parmiter; pages 6 and 36/7: Nigel Downer, Planet Earth Pictures; page 110/11: John Downer, Planet Earth Pictures; page 115: Robert A. Jureit, Planet Earth Pictures.

RSNC

The Royal Society for Nature Conservation is pleased to endorse these excellent, fully illustrated pocket guide books which provide invaluable information on the wildlife of Britain and Northern Europe. Royalties from each book sold will go to help the RSNC's network of 48 Wildlife Trusts and over 50 Urban Wildlife Groups, all working to protect rare and endangered wildlife and threatened habitats. The RSNC and the Wildlife Trusts have a combined membership of 184,000 and look after over 1,800 nature reserves. If you would like to find out more, please contact RSNC, The Green, Whitham Park, Lincoln, LN5 7NR, Telephone 0522 752326.

Bibliography

A small field guide to the molluscs of three major faunal areas in the northern hemisphere will cover just a few of the thousands of known species. This bibliography will lead you to major reference books and specialized monographs that deal with certain families. Annual listings of the world's literature on molluscs is cross-referenced by subject matter in *The Zoological Record*, section 9 on *Mollusca*, London and Philadelphia.

Northeastern Pacific

Abbott, R. Tucker 1974, *American Seashells.* 2nd ed., 663 pp., (about 3000 figs), Van Nostrand Reinhold, New York.

Bernard, F. R. 1979, Bivalve Mollusks of the Western Beaufort Sea [Alaska]. In *Sci. Nat. Hist. Mus. Los Angeles Co.*, no. 313, pp. 1-80, (109 figs).

Bernard, F. R. 1983, *Catalogue of the Living Bivalvia of the Eastern Pacific Ocean: Bering Strait to Cape Horn.* Canadian Special Publ. Fish. Aquat. Sci., vol. 61, 102 pp.

MacGinitie, N. 1959, Marine Mollusca of Point Barrow, Alaska. *Proc. U.S. Nat. Mus.*, vol. 109, pp. 59-208.

McLean, James H. 1969, *Marine Shells of Southern California.* 104 pp., (illus.), Los Angeles County Mus. Nat. Hist., Zoology no. 11, Los Angeles.

Rice, Thomas C. 1968, *A Checklist of the Marine Gastropods from the Puget Sound Region.* 169 pp. Of Sea and Shore Publ., Port Gamble, Washington.

Western Atlantic

Abbott, R. Tucker, 1974, *American Seashells.* 2nd ed., 663 pp., (24 pls, 3000 text figs), Van Nostrand Reinhold Co., New York.

Abbott, R. Tucker, 1986, *Seashells of North America.* Revised ed., 280 pp., (illus.), Golden Press, New York.

Bousefield, E. L. 1960, *Canadian Atlantic Shells.* 72 pp. National Mus. Ottawa, Canada.

Clench, William J., (ed.) 1941-74, *Johnsonia* - Monographs of the Marine Mollusks of the Western Atlantic, vols. 1-5, nos. 1-50. Harvard Univ., Cambridge, Massachusetts.

Eastern Atlantic

Ankel, W. E. 1936, Prosobranchia. In *Die Tierwelt der Nord- und Ostsee.* Vol, IX bl. Akadem. Verlagsgesell., Leipzig.

Bouchet, P, Danrigal, F. and Huyghens, C. 1978, *Coquillage des Côtes atlantiques et de la Manche.* Editions du Pacifique, Paris.

Fretter, V. and Graham. A. 1962, *British Prosobranch Molluscs.* 755 pp. Ray Society, London.
Graham, Alastair 1988, *Molluscs: Prosobranch and Pyramidellid Gastropods.* 2nd ed. 662 pp., (276 text figs). E. J. Brill/Dr. W. Backhuys, Leiden.
McMillan, Nora F. 1968, *British Shells.* 196 pp., (80 pls.-32 in colour, 144 illus.pgs). Frederick Warne & Co., London and New York.
Nordsieck, Fritz 1968-69, *Die europaischen Meeresmuscheln* (vol. 1, Prosobranchia; vol. 2, Bivalvia; vol. 3, Opisthobranchia). G. Fischer, Stuttgart.
Parenzan, Pietro 1970-76, *Carta d'identita delle conchiglie del Mediterraneo.* Vol. 1 Gastropdoi; vol. 2, pts 1 and 2, Bivalvi. Ed. Bios Taras, Taranto.
Tebble, Norman 1976, *British Bivalve Seashells.* 2nd ed. 212 pp., (12 pls, 110 text figs). Royal Scottish Mus., Edinburgh.
Thompson, T. E. and Brown, G. H. 1976, *British Opisthobranch Molluscs.* 203 pp. Synopses of the British Fauna (New Series), no. 8. Academic Press, London and New York.
van Benthem Jutting, W. S. S. 1959, The Netherlands as an environment for molluscan life. *Basteria*, vol. 23, supplement, 174 pp. Leiden.

General and Special Groups

Breisch, L. L. and Kennedy, V. S. 1980, *A Selected Bibliography of Worldwide Oyster Literature.* 309 pp. Univ. Maryland, Maryland.
Kaas, P. and Van Belle, R. A. 1980, *Catalogue of Living Chitons.* 144 pp. E. J. Brill/Dr. W. Backhuys, Leiden.
Kaas, P. and Van Belle, R. A. 1985-87, *Monograph of Living Chitons.* Vols. 1-3. E. J. Brill/ Dr. W. Backhuys, Leiden.
Lalli, Carol M. and Gilmer, Ronald W. 1989, *Pelagic Snails: The Biology of Holoplanktonic Gastropod Mollusks.* 259 pp., (76 text figs). Stanford University Press, California.
Moore, R. C. (ed.). 1960-69, *Treatise on Invertebrate Paleontology.* Part I (Gastropoda), Part N, vols. 1 and 2 (Bivalvia). Geol. Soc. America, Boulder, Colorado.
Morton, J. E. 1976, *Molluscs.* 4th ed. 244 pp., (41 text figs). Hutchinson & Co., London.
Thompson, T. E. 1976, *Biology of Opisthobranch Molluscs.* Vol. 1, 207 pp. Ray Society, London.
Thompson, T. E. and Brown, G. H. 1984, *Biology of Opisthobranch Molluscs.* Vol. 2, 229 pp. (41 coloured pls), Ray Society, London.
Turner, Ruth D. 1966, *A Survey and Illustrated Catalogue of the Teredinidae.* 265 pp., (64 pls), Mus. Comp. Zool., Harvard Univ., Cambridge, Massachusetts.
Yonge, C. M. and Thompson, T. E. 1976, *Living Marine Molluscs.* 288 pp., (16 pls, 162 text figs). Collins, London.

Index